Straight Ahead!

Encouragement for the Journey

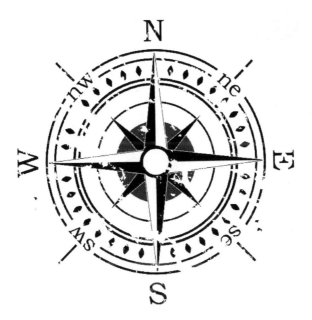

A 60 Day Devotional

Joel Tetreau

STRAIGHT AHEAD
Encouragement for the Journey A 60 Day Devotional

Scripture quotations (unless otherwise noted) are taken from the New American Standard Bible © 1960, 1962, 1963, 1968, 1971, 1972, 1973, 1975, 1977, 1995 by The Lockman Foundation. Used by permission (www.Lockman.org)

Straight-Ahead Publishing
Cover by Rossano Designs

I dedicate this 60 day devotional, "Straight Ahead! - Encouragement for the Journey," to my best friend, partner in life and ministry, wife and mother of my children — Toni Lee Carmack Tetreau.

Toni — thanks for being God's tool of encouragement for the darkest seasons of life. You are the GPS in my directions, the breath in my lungs, the sanity in my head, and the truest love of my life. I'm so thankful for your steady hand on my heart and in our home.

"You will not see anyone who is truly striving after his spiritual advancement who is not given to spiritual reading."
Athanasius of Alexandria

"It is the nature of faith to believe God upon His bare word... It will not be, saith sense; it cannot be, saith reason; it both can and will be, saith faith, for I have a promsie."
John Trapp

"We fear men so much, because we fear God so little. One cures another. When man's terror scares you, turn your thoughts to the wrath of God."
William Gurnall

"Hope fills the afflicted soul with such inward joy and consolation, that it can laugh while tears are in the eye, sign and sing all in a breath; it is called "the rejoicing of hope" (Hebrews 3:6).
William Gurnall

Table of Contents

Forward

In the early 2000's, we saw the breakout phenomena known as reality TV. People allowed themselves and their lives to be continuously recorded and aired for everyone to see. It seemed that much of this was billed as "real life", yet, in many cases, it was staged to create certain scenarios and situations. It seemed that reality TV bred suspicion and leeriness that things were not always as they seemed. This gave way to the phenomena known as "fake news." We went from TV shows that were supposed to be real and raw, to shows we couldn't really trust, to now nothing can be trusted as real--including our news. So, what are we to do?

Joel Tetreau has given us a respite from the fake and staged world we now live in with his devotional on life and leadership. He combines his almost 30 years of ministry leadership experience with practical, real-life applications of those truths. Yet, in a style that is uniquely Joel's, he does it in a real and raw manner. The best way to read these devotionals is to imagine that you are chillin' with Joel at a coffee shop or restaurant and you and Joel are just two friends who are talking real with each other. Joel offers these devotionals in a non-presumptive, non-pretentious manner. They are real, down-to-earth, and practical just like Joel himself.

This devotional will be an excellent resource for you as you lead the people God has called you to lead--whether that is your family, your children, your co-workers, people in your church, or people in your community. The thoughts and the principles from God's word that Joel presents will make you laugh, will make you think, but most importantly will point you to Christ. So, grab your favorite drink, read the text, read Joel's thoughts, and ask God to help you become the leader He wants you to be. I trust that this book will be an encouragement to you as it has been to me. Joel is your friend and he invites in on the journey of friends in the areas of leadership and life.

Dr. Dave Deets

Lead Pastor, Whitneyville Bible Church, Caledonia (Grand Rapids), MI

Author, *Selecting Elders: A Biblical Guide to Choosing God's Shepherds*

Midwest Regional Coordinator, Institute of Biblical Leadership, Fairview, NC

Preface

I am thankful to present this 60 day devotional for your personal study and daily consideration. You will notice that the devotional, while hopefully sourced in a careful grasp of God's Word, is not so loaded down with theological terminology as to scare the average Christian away. It is put together with a hope that the Scriptural concepts found here can give us real encouragement as we labor together in the corner of the Lord's vineyard which His grace has placed us.

Perhaps my favorite Bible character in the Scriptures is Barnabas. Barnabas was not the loud-mouth that Paul probably could be. He wasn't the first to jump out of the boat like was Peter. He wasn't even the closest to Jesus like John "the Beloved" was. Barnabas was the leader in the early church who sought out to simply encourage God's children and especially other leaders.

My prayer is that *Straight Ahead: Encouragement for the Journey* will encourage your heart as Barnabas did for the early church. I'm hopeful that this can be a help to both leaders in life and ministry, as well as those who simply wish to follow God through the next section of life's journey. The study of God's Word is vital to the growth and stability of the believer. Over my twenty-five plus years of ministry, perhaps the most important priority, as it relates to those with whom I minister, is their spiritual growth and walk with the Lord. There really is nothing in ministry more important than *"feeding God's sheep"* (John 21:15). When Jesus sent out "the

Twelve" (Matthew 10), you notice the great compassion for His children. Many were lost, "weary and scattered, like sheep having no shepherd" (Matthew 9:36).

God's Word is important because it is infallible (that is, without error.) Proverbs 30:5-6 explains that His revelation is pure and, as such, it becomes the ultimate shield for we who place our trust in God. Second, the Scriptures are important because they are sufficient for our needs. 2 Timothy 3:16-17 explains that the Word benefits us in our walk with God. Third, the Bible is authoritative. Fourth, it is directive (Psalm 119:105). Fifth, the cannon is complete! Revelation 22 explains that those who try to add revelation to the completed text of Scripture are actually giving false prophecy. God's Word is complete and all we need for faith and righteousness (2 Peter 1:3). All Scriptural references throughout this devotional are taken from the NASB unless otherwise specified.

The ultimate aim for this devotional is to remind us all who Jesus of Nazareth actually is. He is our Lord! Our Captain is King Jesus. He knows exactly where we are and exactly where we're going! He's designed the trip and determined its end. Straight Ahead!

1

It's Never Too Late

"Now Moses was pasturing the flock of Jethro his father-in-law, the priest of Median; and he led the flock to the west side of the wilderness, and came to Horeb, the mountain of God. And the Angel of the LORD appeared to him in a blazing fire from the midst of a bush..." (Ex. 3:1-2a)

So many of us are looking at a new chapter of life and we're thinking, "Okay, God, so why did I have to wait a year, or five years, or ten years, until I was ready for this!?" Consider Moses--he was eighty and still watching his wife's dad's sheep! How does that go down at the sixty-year high school reunion!?

So, Moses, what have you been doing ever since you left the royal family? Oh, you watch 'fluffy' on the back side of the Midian desert.

So, the answer in part is: God's timing is intentional. It is never too early or too late.

Another way to look at this is to recognize that maybe we just weren't ready yet. Look, some of those years you think were wasted, simply weren't. God was teaching you about

Him, about you, and probably giving you insight that you will now use on a regular basis. God typically has to teach His followers certain navigational tools for the rougher parts of the journey.

It's interesting to consider what God's servants were doing when God explained what the rest of the journey would be for them. Moses was leading Jethro's sheep near Mt. Horeb.

And consider the genesis of David's leadership and ministry.

After the death of King Saul, God told Samuel to go and anoint one of the sons of Jesse as king (1 Sam. 16). After passing up seven of Jesse's sons, they had to go find the youngest of the family. It's clear the family didn't think David would have a chance. Well, God knew something no one else would have guessed. David was a man after "God's own heart." This is why God wanted to annoint him as king.

Once again, consider what David was doing. He was out and away from the center of the action, also watching his father's sheep. Note the pattern!

Earlier, during the time of the Judges, we read in Judges 6 that Gideon was threshing wheat in his father's winepress. He was doing so to stay out of the eye of the Midianites. The Bible reader has to be as shocked as Gideon heard the angel greet him with these words, *"The LORD is with you, O valiant warrior."*

Valiant warrior? Who? Gideon?

What is remarkable about God is that He often sees far more potential in us than we see in ourselves. He sees that because He's the One who put it in us in the first place!

I suppose this characteristic of God impacts me at a deep level when it shows up in the lives of friends, family members, and mentors. I'm reminded of my parents, my wife, and my friends who have never given up on me. I'm thankful for teachers (like John Pinkerton, Jr. High English teacher) who saw potential in me that even I didn't see! His encouragement turned me into a reader. I have a long list of coaches and, later in life, mentors who encouraged my development of leadership "under fire."

Some of us, like Moses, have had difficult experiences in our past and thus it's difficult for us to imagine that God could use us. But Joel 2:25 reminds me that God can make up for *"the years of locusts."* Besides, God doesn't measure usefulness by the passage of time. Jesus had three years of ministry. That's it. He lived 30 years before He officially began His three-year-long ministry and yet He accomplished all that He needed to accomplish.

God has tailored and orchestrated a plan for your life. In Ephesians 1:11 tells us, *"...also we have obtained an inheritance, having been predestined according to His purpose who works all things after the counsel of His will..."*

If you have time, you might read the rest of chapter three and into chapter four of Exodus. Moses gives all the excuses as to why he isn't ready. God doesn't allow any of it to fly. So, when God brings you that new opportunity, that new season, and you are discouraged because you think you're late to the party, consider that God is never late. He knew what you needed to go through before you could effectively steward the new season in front of you.

Straight Ahead my friends! JT

2

Wisdom and Knowledge

"The fear of the LORD is the beginning of knowledge; fools despise wisdom and instruction." (Prov. 1:7).

There is nothing morally wrong with ignorance. With the amount of "knowable data" doubling on this planet every thirteen months (nanotechnology data doubles even faster), it's simply not possible for any of us to stay up with the growing amount of raw information.

Thankfully the Scriptures put a premium on wisdom, not "facts." Lots of facts often bloat the head, not to mention the ever-inflatable ego. The Latin phrase is *"Scientia infla"* (knowledge puffs up.) Ryan Holiday describes a twisted ego as, "an unhealthy belief in our own importance" (Ryan Holiday, *Ego is the Enemy*). The Scriptures explain that foolishness, not ignorance, is dangerous for your walk!

I have a friend who has served in a counseling ministry for years. One of the things he has noted is that Christians, especially those who went to Christian school or Christian college or even spent years in Sunday School, try to impress you with the amount of "data" they know. I have been with him in several sessions when he looked at the believer and would say, "yeah, one of your problems is that you know a lot!" Over the years of church and leadership ministry I've noted even Christian leaders can swallow the self-diluted Kool-Aid that "they know." Some have called this the "Messiah Syndrome." (Because I'm the man of God, my perspective on just about everything is always right.) Oh my word! I have never been able to understand how God's people put up with such nonsense.

In the particular ecclesiastical community I grew up in, one of the things that was heavily emphasized was a recognition of and separation from error. The exception was if "error" was clearly found in your own leadership. Well, then you were taught that even if the authority is wrong, it's right. That's confusion and, while it can be seen with honorable intentions, this is a misunderstanding of the Scripture's teaching on authority. It's one thing for a leader to make a mistake in a decision. All leaders will fail from time to time. However, when a leader has a pattern of sinful and arrogant leadership patterns, that leader must be confronted by other leaders and, if the behavior, attitude, or incorrect doctrine is not corrected, removed. The result of that blinded approach to leadership has been the shipwreck of countless young people that grew up in the Christian School movement and conservative gospel preaching churches that have run away from the faith in no small relation to the gross hypocrisy they saw in leadership and a twisted "handbook" approach to Christianity.

The problem was not "Church" or even a "Christian School" per se. The issues were related to a twisted view of leadership and sanctification. Too many leaders presented man-made institutional policy as if it were evidence of a heart of righteousness. I guess they missed Jesus' teaching on the Pharisees! The problem with many ecclesiastical associations of ministry is they encourage a "Pyramid and the Box" approach to ministry that essentially keeps them removed from Biblical accountability. In the book I wrote on decision-making in the church, I noted these and other characteristics of what I affectionately call, *"the dictator"* or in some cases, *"the monarchy."* In this book I noted that one of the extremes found in ministry decision-making is the one leader who is really not accountable to anyone. He (or she) acts like they are the Pharaoh on top of their own pyramid. It was Lord Acton who noted the axiom, "power corrupts, absolute power corrupts absolutely." (Tetreau, Joel. *Pyramid and the Box: The Decision-Making Process in a Local New Testament Church*, Wipf and Stock Publishers, 2013.) In 3 John, Diotrephes was a leader who typifies this kind of poisoned attitude.

Back to a fool. A fool is not a fool because he doesn't know. A fool is a fool because he lacks restraint. A clear example is the mouth. Solomon refers to this person as *"a babbling fool"* (Prov. 10:8). His mouth, *"spouts folly"* (Prov. 15:2). Some of us take pride in that we just say what we think, so there! (I think we had a fair amount of this in the recent election cycle and since). So does a fool! *"A fool does not delight in understanding, but only in revealing his own mind."* (Prov. 18:2). If you notice a growing number of God-loving people keeping you at arm's length, perhaps you need to ask yourself, "have I grown into the shoes of a fool?" Why would the righteous avoid you? Well, Solomon notes, *"it's better to meet a bear robbed of her cubs than a fool in his folly"* (Prov. 17:12). Don't become a fool, my friend.

Straight Ahead, JT

3

Light When it's Dark

"For Thou art my lamp, O LORD; and the LORD illlumines my darkness." (2 Sam. 22:29)

Are you or a loved-one in a "dark place?" Christian people love the beloved Psalmist, King David, for many reasons. One is because of his writings found in the testimony of Scripture. So many of his Psalms are raw with real-life experience and emotion. You cannot miss the parallel between 2 Samuel 22 and Psalm 18. David knew about dealing with life when it "turned dark." Consider the darkness of personal family trauma, the darkness of a crazed angry, envious, or jealous boss (the kind who try to nail you to the wall, literally)! The darkness of living with a spouse who hates you all the time! Consider the darkness of personal moral failure that goes viral. Consider the darkness of physical illness or mental and emotional struggles such as anxiety or deep depression. Consider the darkness of bitter loss...like the violent death of not one...but several children. Consider losing the "dearest-one" of your life and not being able to say or do a thing to stop them from walking out of your life--forever. David had all of this, yet David was able to turn to God as his lamp because he knew that God would bring His light into David's darkness.

We all have seasons of darkness. In 1662, the Act of Uniformity required Puritan churches in England to swear a kind of uhealthy, "Rome-like" allegiance to the Church of England. Nearly two thousand clergy refused, all of whom were ejected from their Church of England office on St. Bartholomew's Day, August 24, 1662. Nonconformist clergy experienced decades of suffering until the "Toleration Act" of 1689. While that season was miserable for dear English Puritans, it also gave birth to some of the most powerful extant Puritan writings to date (John Bunyan, Richard Baxter, etc...). One can go to nonconformist's graves in New England, Massachusetts, and London and see the markers of men and women who paid the price for faithfulness to God. The result of their lives shone the light of the Gospel in such a way that it impacted multitudes who were in darknenss.

The constant reality for God's children is that we live in a place that is not our home. We live under the shadow of depravity and the curse, which means we live in a dark world with dark people, enslaved by dark hearts. How does the light of God work in that kind of a context? We are told that when (prophetically & practically) God shows up, darkness remains *"under His feet"* (2 Sam. 22:10). This is because the light of God's will, His Word, and work is so very bright when we submit to God's way. I love the contrast of Moses glowing after being in the presence of God (Ex. 34:29-30). The same thing occurred with Jesus, Moses, and Elijah when clothed in brilliant glory on the Mountain in Mt. 17. It may have been Mount Herman because of its location near Caesarea Philippi

(Mt. 17:1-4). When we are able by faith to see the light of hope even in the face of darkness, it energizes our faith. On the "Mount of Transfiguration" it so energized Peter, I think he perhaps needed oxygen—Peter, Let's build three tabernacles!

No, we are too often like Elijah's servant in Dothan (2 Kings 6) who could not see that the army of God's light had the mountains surrounded. I love the prophet's instruction to his servant when thinking of the dark invaders in light of the armies of heaven: "*stop fearing!*" God's light kills darkness like sunshine kills a dark fog as it rises out of the east plowing towards its westward route.

Going back to King David, we note that the basis of David's deliverance was a humble attitude towards God, even when He failed. Maybe you are in a dark place. For the last thirty years, I've been thrilled to travel the globe encouraging Christian leaders, many of them in dark places. I've been with them in war torn places. I've been with them where the government has outlawed or severely restricted religious freedom. In a couple of places I've done ministry, it probably wasn't safe to do ministry. What I've noted is that when God's children minister when and where it's dark, the contrast to the Gospel of Christ is an unmistakable brilliance that brings hope. So as God's children, we will find ourself in an occasional dark place.

Just remember. He's not in a dark place (Ps. 139:12)! He is the Light that penetrates the darkest of hours. God bless you, my friend. There is hope!

Straight Ahead JT

4

Honoring Parents

"Then he went up from there to Bethel; and as he was going up the way, young lads came out from the city and mocked him and said to him, 'Go up, you baldhead; go up, you baldhead! When he looked behind him and saw them, he cursed them in the name of the LORD. Then two female bears came out of the woods and tore up forty-two lads of their number." (2 Ki. 2:23-24).

Life is short. Want to make it shorter? Go ahead and be dishonorable to your parents or those spiritual and civil leaders that God has put in your life. Make that a habit and you'll die early!

Here, a group of adolescents were mocking God's servant Elisha. God apparently didn't appreciate anyone disrespecting His prophets. I struggle to have mercy in my heart for those who treat their parents and those in spiritual authority badly--even as adults. You don't have to agree with everything they say or believe and you don't have to respond if or when they are difficult as they age. You can choose to rise above their struggles and love them at the same time.

Consider (Eph. 6:2) "*Honor your father and mother (which is the first commandment with a promise.)*"

I place the blame of many wayward adolescents on the shoulders of parents who handed over their parenting responsibility to the children themselves. Proverbs 22:15 explains "*Foolishness is bound up in the heart of a child.*" I've shuddered when I've heard a parent say, "well, we want the child to choose for himself." I really want to say, "friend, you are confused!" That's why God gave your child, parents! What's sad is that once a child has worked his way through the transition into adulthood, there lately has been a clear amount of confusion on the baton handoff. There are ministry leaders that, in teaching young people the principle of "leaving and cleaving", are essentially encouraging "ignoring, disrespecting, and slamming" mom and dad to their face or behind their back. Even if your parents are not honoring the "first-level" priority you are to have with your spouse, there is an honorable way of dealing with them on those issues.

A final note for adolescents who are habitually irresponsible at home, school, work, church, etc.... I'm not sure what to tell you, kid. The Bible doesn't tell us much about how to deal with your type because usually you would have already been stoned by now (Dt. 21:18-21). Soon you'll need to pay for your own gas, car, food, housing, cell phone, bed, clothes, etc. All of this means you'll need to hold down a job that pays more than minimum wage. So, if I were you, I'd stop acting like an idiot (the proverbial word is "fool") and I would do my school work, do my part to be productive, and cooperate at home. Be responsible at your minimum wage job. If you don't even work, go get a "wee little job" to start out. If none of this makes sense, join the army (if they will take you.) The military will help you with everything, like how to put your shirt on, when to hike, when to sleep, how to make your bed, etc. If you think this note is cruel, you have no idea how your path is headed straight into a cruel world you are not prepared to handle. Get it together, my friend.

Straight Ahead, JT

5

What can you do?

"But Joseph said to them, 'Do not be afraid, for am I in God's place? And as for you, you meant evil against me, but God meant it for good in order to bring about this present result, to preserve man people alive." (Gen. 50:19-20)

I love the character of Joseph found in the later parts of Genesis. In Genesis 37, Joseph, at the age of 17, is sold into slavery by his brothers, who admittedly were leaning towards taking his life. A story was made-up that Joseph had been killed by some ferocious beast. To make the story believable, his siblings tore his coat of many colors and dipped it in goat's blood. His only crime was that he was his father's favorite and he had a tendency to dream and share those dreams with his envious brothers.

In Genesis 39, Joseph went to prison despite being innocent of the crime for which he was falsely accused by Mrs. Potiphar. In Genesis 40, even after giving the royal cupbearer the good news he would survive his imprisonment, unlike the unfortunate chap who led the royal baking team, the cup-bearer forgot to speak on Joseph's behalf after receiving his life-giving freedom. Joseph remained in prison for an unjust cause. What's clear is that all of this was actually part of God's plan and God was with him every step of the way.

Most of us will experience our own joy-crushing event(s) in life as God builds us up for our ultimate purpose for being here. The worst thing in the world might be to experience a bit of success too early in life. If you've been able to achieve a thing or two, just know that this is the result of God's mercy. As soon as you become puffed up with the pride of your early success, you are doomed to be blinded by an ego trip that shipwrecks you on the mirage of past victory. Richard Feyman noted, "you must not fool yourself - and you are the easiest person to fool." Those whose impact really outlives their own life are the few who care far more about "making a difference" and doubt the lasting value of "making a name." Most of the world's popular people are masters at marketing themselves and, frankly, they too often are made up of cheap plastic. You know that because when the heat is on, they melt.

Joseph just plows on, making the best of prison. When we find ourself "incarcerated" in a tough season, the challenge will usually not end by you bending the bars of life. There is an interesting concept found in Galatians 4:19 that has helped me in the midst of ministry when it gets tough. Paul explains that in order for Christ to be "formed" in God's children, humanly speaking, it will require him to experience something like "birth pangs" before he can impact the spiritual life and development of those in his ministry. So if that is true of our mentors, imagine the struggle that sometimes requires us to become conformed to the image of His Son. (See Gordon D. Fee, *Pauline Christology*, Hendrickson Publishers, p. 231). Just focus on the things you can do. To make the biggest difference we must care far more for our "mission" and far less for our "reputation." We struggle with this in large part because of human nature.

Straight Ahead friends! JT

6

God's Role for the Individual

"For consider your calling, brethren, that there were not many wise according to the flesh, not many mighty, not many noble; but God has chosen the foolish things of the world to shame the wise, and God has chosen the weak things of the world to shame the things which are strong..." (1 Cor. 1:26-27).

God uses "we who are weak and struggle" so He receives glory. Around 432 AD, a previously little known missionary from Britain landed in Ireland. He had been the son of Christian parents but had spent an earlier part of his life on the island as a slave. Determined to go back, Patrick made a lasting impact for the cause of Christ. It is estimated that some 300 churches and 120,000 baptized believers were the result of Patrick's ministry. Patrick used a simple teaching technique to reach the pagans of Ireland with the message of Jesus. An example of that was how he used the shamrock as a teaching tool for the doctrine of the Trinity. Paul explains that God chooses the "little known" to accomplish His work.

We often think, "What can *I* do?" We think "I'm not a person of God like Peter, James, John, Andrew, Philip, Bartholomew, Matthew, Thomas, James, Thaddeus, or Simon the Zealot."

First, this group was hardly consistently "stellar." The list of leaders in the Old Testament doesn't get much better apart from grace. Second, remember that God changed these leaders in time (after they had witnessed the resurrection and been indwelt by the Holy Spirit and Jesus had gone back to heaven). He molds and transforms all of His followers. Third, consider that God takes men and women who struggle, and if they will "believe on the Lord" (not just for salvation), and if they will "act on their faith," God can and will transform them into something of a hero. (John MacArthur, *Twelve Unlikely Heroes*, Thomas Nelson Publishers, p. XI).

I have a list of personal heroes who have had the courage to stand up for what was right even though many around them were entrenched in a kind of blind traditionalism.

One individual whom I have tremendous historic respect for was Rosa Parks. In December of 1955, Rosa refused to give up her seat up to a white passenger on a city bus in Montgomery, Alabama. Rosa was not a law-maker, or a person with a large reach of influence. No, Rosa Parks was a seamstress who had grown tired of just giving in to what she believed was morally wrong. Her conviction of justice was on display even as a child. On one occasion, Rosa picked up a brick to challenge a white bully. Rosa told her grandmother, "I would rather be lynched than live to be mistreated and not be allowed to say, 'I don't like it.'"[1] Even though Rosa was sitting in the designated areas for African-Americans to sit, the bus driver instructed Rosa to move back because additional whites were coming onto the bus and he knew that they would not be willing to sit behind an African-American. Rosa decided then and there, this would be her day. Her act of principled defiance resulted in a bus boycott which aided the momentum of the Civil Rights Movement in the United States. The immediate impact was difficult for her. She lost her job and received numerous death threats. Looking back on the event, it is unmistakable to note how her courage aided in the ending of a variety of egregious laws and practices of inequality that plagued many in the South and throughout the country. So the principle is this, you don't have to be larger than life to make an impact that is larger than your life!

Here is a reminder that some of the largest accommodations made by faithful servants received little mention in the New Testament. Perhaps you are simply a disciple, a lover, and follower of Jesus. A helper who serves as you can and whose day job includes things like parenting, cooking, or "punching a time clock" (like Cleopas, Joanna, Mary the mother of Jesus, Mary of Bethany, Mary Magdalene, Salome, and Susanna). Perhaps you serve as "just a deacon" (like Philip the missionary/evangelist, Phoebe, or Steven the martyr). Perhaps you just "help out" in some other form of ministry (like Timothy, Titus, Tychius, Philemon, and Epaphras [who may be the same as Epaphroditus], Aristarchus, Silas, or Barnabas). Here's the point. God's Kingdom, Christ' Body, and the Church of Jesus desperately

---

1 "50 Decisions that Changed The World" (*History Revealed* - Christmas 2017 Edition.)

needs you to simply serve Jesus in your corner of the Lord's vineyard, "as He has gifted you!" Simplicity of service in God's call is in fact heroic. In the final analysis, the only significance any of us have is wrapped up in the phrase, "in Christ."

Straight Ahead my friends! JT

7

Pressing Forward

"...but one thing I do: forgetting what lies behind and reaching forward to what lies ahead, I press on toward the goal for the prize of the upward call of God in Christ Jesus." (Phil. 3:13b-14a)

Some things we simply will never know and that's OK because we don't have to know in order to trust God. If you are here, it is because God has a job for you to do. *"Your life is short, your duties many, your assistance great and your reward sure; therefore faint not, hold on and hold up, in ways of well-doing, and heaven shall make amends for all."* (Thomas Brooks)

If there is a common frustration that can stop our effectiveness in the realm of family, work, and even ministry, it is being hit with the overwhelming feeling of "loss" or the sense that we are "lost." Both are normal, and both can be overcome by having a renewed sense of direction. A quick trip through history will reveal that you can win the battle and still lose the war. Or you can lose the battle and win the war.

Frankly, General George Washington lost a surprising number of smaller battles throughout the War of Independence but pulled off the victory of the ages as the North American colonials won their independence against the world's 18th century superpower, Great Britain. Washington knew that if his army just kept living, kept bleeding the British, with the help of a continued restocked local army (or the French), that eventually the odds would be in his favor and allow him to push the advantage against Cornwallis. The result of that strategy was Yorktown and victory.

The Apostle Paul in Philippians 3 reminds us that he was reaching forward to those things (several different goals) all of which were attached to one over-arching chief goal (the upward call of God in Christ Jesus). So, it is important that we spend significant time in listening to God through faith, His Word, and prayer to understand what my/your role is in our Lord's "vineyard work." So, as I understand this, then I can have a compass bearing that encourages a renewed direction. When I'm clear on direction, I can work beyond those distractions of temporary "loss" and "feeling lost."

A surface view of Scripture will reveal an impressive list of saints who at times were "fuzzy" on direction--consider Abraham, Joseph, Elijah, David, Moses, Jonah, Isaiah, Jeremiah, Paul, Peter, and Mary to name just a few. So how do you find that renewed direction? We typically become stuck when we are focused on what we do not know. Forget that! What *do* you know? Start with what God has revealed and go there. In route, God will provide all the clarity you need.

I love the example we have from Genesis 24:27. The servant of Abraham, reflecting on how God had led him to

Mesopotamia in order find the wife of Isaac, Rebekah, said: *"as for me, the LORD has guided me in the way to the house of my master's brothers."* The servant did not wait first to get directions before starting off on his journey. Instead, as he was on his way, he trusted that the LORD would guide his footsteps. Often, we will never be given a roadmap or detailed instructions and that's okay--because we don't need these in order to trust God. If you are here, there, or wherever, it is because God has a job for you to do. So, in the words of the well-known football coach, Bill Belichick, "do your job!"

Straight Ahead, my friends! JT

8

Being Plastic

"Pride goes before destruction, and a haughty spirit before stumbling." (Prov. 16:18).

From the time I was in pee-wee baseball until the end of high school, I often played catcher. It helped that I was short and stocky. I remember on several occasions in high school baseball not being able to throw out the runner at second base in time. On one memorable occasion in my junior year, we were playing a school that was larger than ours and several of their players had stolen second base consecutively. The team tasted blood and so they began to taunt. The star of the team made it to first and so one of his buddies yelled out, *"You got this 'Carl Lewis!'"* The pitch came and, without aiming, I simply fired the ball as fast as I could in the general direction of second base. Imagine the shock and delight when my ball made it to my second baseman just ahead of "Carl," where the umpire called the would-be olympian "out!" At that point in time, I think I experienced just a taste of the feeling when David's stone found the strategic location in the Philistine's forehead. My buddy Cameron Bunt who was on the receiving end of the throw on second base and who had the delightful task of tagging the base-runner out, jumped up and down and shouted out "Carl Lewis is thrown out at second base!" I can still see Cameron's silly smile in my head. My team mates rushed me like I had won the World Series. It was a memory I'll never forget. Don't miss the point. Pride often preceedes an out for all of us. Pride is also a characteristic of people who are what I call "plastic."

I've always been amazed by the use of plastic. In 1927, DuPont began to work with a substance known at the time as "Fiber66." After twelve years of unrelenting work and 27 million dollars of investment and research, the pioneers of the plastic industry were able to commercially refine nylon. The rest, as they say, "is history." Over the last seventy plus years, plastic and its cousin rubber has been used for endless applications. The English word "plastic" comes from the Greek "plastikos" meaning, "capable of being shaped or molded." The thing about plastic is that there are all kinds of helpful things you can do with it. Plastic today has replaced many things that once were made of leather, paper, metal, glass, wood, stone, etc. There is a limitation with plastic. Once it is molded, it takes an unbelievable amount of heat to melt it and re-form it. An additional negative with plastic is that when combined with other elements, it is often toxic. One of my main disappointments in life is to see good people become tricked and mesmerized by what I call, "plastic people." In some sad cases, good people have become plastic themselves in no small part because the company with which they've decided to spend their time.

People who are plastic are not real. They are surface. They have molded themselves around concepts of what is "cool." One of the chief characteristics of "the plastics" is that they get their kicks out of putting other people down. Frankly, once you get past their shallow surface, you typically find out all that's left with this people-group is wax! The Scripture warns us about the dangers of becoming plastic and thus toxic to even ourselves. In Ephesians 4:2 we read, "*With all humility and gentleness, with patience, showing forbearance to one another in love,...*" The Apostle Paul reminds us in Romans 12:16, "*Be of the same mind toward one another; do not be haughty in mind, but associate with the lowly. Do not be wise in your own estimation.*" A great verse, especially for gals who are tempted to "go plastic", is found in 1 Peter 3:3-4, "*And let not your adornment be merely external—braiding the hair, and wearing gold jewelry, or putting on dresses; but let it be the hidden person of the heart, with the imperishable quality of a gente and quiet spirit, which is precious in the sight of God.*"

Jesus explains to His servants that if you are going to be effective with a Kingdom of God mindset, "If *anyone who wants to be first,he shall be last of all, and servant of all.*" (Mk. 9:35). Well, you can see it's just easier to be plastic! The good news is if you are plastic, God might still use you. The bad news is that He will have to put you in the fire to melt you and make you into something better. Typically, that process is not pleasant. When God puts us through "plastic surgery," that usually corresponds with life-altering crises. Maybe we should humble ourselves so God doesn't have to. May God give us all the grace to be real...not plastic.

Straight Ahead! JT

9

Empty Excuses

"I wrote something to the church; but Diotrephes, who loves to be first among them, does not accept what we say. For this reason, if I come, I will call attention to his deeds which he does, unjustly accusing us with wicked words; and not satisfied with this, neither does he himself receive the brethren, and he forbids those who desire to do so, and puts them out of the church." (3 John 9-10).

Scripture gives a long list of the wrong kind of leaders (Diotrephes in 3 John, Jezebel in the O.T.) There are two kinds of wrong leaders. The first kind of "wrong leader" is the kind who has been able, through leadership organizational politics, to wiggle or buy their way into an office or position. However, their leadership is only on paper. Just because a person is in authority over others, does not mean they are a leader. Not being a natural or organic leader, they must resort to threats, manipulation, and bullying tactics. They have to snort and shout and bang and threaten through coercion to get things done. That is, they have no natural or organic leadership skills. The best leaders are those who simply lead and people follow--not because they have to, but because they want to.

A second kind of "wrong leader" is the kind who thinks he is qualified for real leadership when he has no experience and has never been successful at that "sort-of" leadership. Antiquity is full of examples of how the "Diotrephes" kind of leaders often sink their own ship. When the Empress Elizabeth of Russia died in 1761, the leadership of the Russian empire fell to her nephew, the Grand Duke, Peter III. History suggests the marriage between Peter and his royal bride, Catherine II was hardly benevolent and that the emperor had designs to rid himself of Catherine one way or another. About six months after Peter's ascension to power, Catherine mobilized troops in St. Petersburg with the resulting assassination of her estranged husband, Peter III. Catherine ruled and expanded the Russian empire over the next 34 years.[2]

Leaders who are real leaders figure out quickly that leadership is not based on idealism. You have to take the good, the bad, and the ugly and try to accomplish the God-given task God has laid in your lap.

In Exodus 3 and 4, Moses argues with God as to why he is not the right kind of leader. Here are some of his excuses:

(1) Who am I? Moses isn't sure he can accomplish anything. He is an ex-con, former member of Egyptian royalty who has for 40 years been "on the run," hiding and living in Midian--so certainly he can't be the right guy!

---

2 "50 Decisions that Changed The World" (*History Revealed* - Christmas 2017 Edition.)

(2) "Who am I?" probably also includes "I can't do it!" God says, "I'll be with you." A leader called of God for a purpose has to (in the words of the Apostle Paul), *"... forgetting what lies behind..."* (Philippians 3:13). At the top of the list of things to forget are those times of failure. We can't afford to forget the lessons of those painful chapters in our life but we also can't allow ourselves to stay in the place of "failure" in our minds either. We have to move on emotionally. In Christ we have victory. Philippians 4:13 reminds us, *"I can do all things through Him who strengthens me."*

(3) Back to Moses. Moses says "but they won't know You, God...how do I explain You to them?" God tells Moses to tell them *"I AM WHO I AM; and He said, thus you shall say to the sons of Israel, I AM has sent me to you."*

(4) Moses says "They won't believe me!" God says "I'll give them proof!" And He does.

(5) Moses continues to try to back out, "I'm not good at public speaking!" God reminds Moses, "I made your mouth, son!"

(6) Finally, we get to the best one of all. Oh God, "can't you just send someone else?!" God's answer is, "No!" I love this passage for so many reasons. It probably is that some of you are not the wrong kind of leader, but the right kind—although reluctant—a Moses. Listen, just go with God and His plan. He will enable you to accomplish what He calls you to do.

Straight Ahead my friend! JT

10

Angry Fathers

"And fathers, do not provoke your children to anger; but bring them up in the discipline and instruction of the LORD." (Eph. 6:4)

An important implication of this text for modern parenting is this: too often, parents of children still living at home and those out on their own have unfair expectations of what their children must do and how their children must succeed to prove their success as parents. So, encouragement is fine, but at some point, when it becomes all about making the parents look good, this kind of thing becomes selfish. It indeed provokes or exasperates our children to the place where, in frustration, many simply "give up." History is full of examples of cruel parents. "Ivan the Terrible" had nine children. History tells us the children suffered years of abuse. In 1581, Ivan beat his pregnant daughter-in-law as punishment for wearing clothing he did not deem appropriate. When Ivan's son (also named Ivan) confronted dad, apparently the czar struck his offspring on the head with his scepter. The younger Ivan died a few days later.

Another history example comes from the Roman emperor Constantine, who ruled from 306 until he died in 337 A.D. At first, the emperor worked closely with his eldest son Crispus, who oversaw many of his father's military campaigns. For some reason, Constantine ordered his son Crispus executed in 326 A.D. His son's name was erased from the official records and monuments that had been dedicated to him were destroyed (*Histories best and worst dads*, www.history.com).

History aside, when the real issue is how the child's success, or failures, impact the parent's image, several things grow out of that. First, this causes the child to feel conflicted as he/she seeks to achieve what he/she wants in life. When the parent tries to prevent this by making it clear that the child is expected to meet the parent's goals and to make the parent "proud", it will lead to frustration, anger, and sometimes outright rebellion or severe depression. Second, it adds unnecessary hardships to the burdens our kids are already facing. Give them time, space, and room to figure it out! The largest impact we can make as parents has much more to do with teaching our children self-control rather than parent control. Remember except for Jesus, all of God's children fail to one degree or another. Perhaps some of us should loosen up a bit?

The take home is simple, if not pointed. If you parent your children without love and mercy, you can expect hate and cruelty from your kids and you will reap what you have sown--multiplied. Perhaps you'll be blessed by forgiving children as I have been. If you choose to parent without love and mercy, don't claim to be Christian in your parenting method. It's something else (like perhaps "Pavlovian Conditioning" that too often passes as Christian parenting). Sure, parenting includes discipline that sometimes looks a lot more like punishment—at least from the child's point of view. But, if that's all you do, that's all you'll get! Discipline focuses on training and teaching. Discipline is very different from punishment. Parents need to focus not on raising a "child." Instead, they need to strive to raise an "adult". With each decision, from infancy forward, the parent needs to ask: how can this moment teach or help move my child toward adulthood? The good news for your children is that God can redeem your parenting failures and give your kids other parents...adopted and others. God is merciful to the merciful (Mt. 5:7). Be merciful to your loved-ones...especially to your children. Life will be better.

Straight Ahead! JT

11

Think, Then Speak

"....But let everyone be quick to hear, slow to speak and slow to anger." (James 1:19)

The saying goes, "it's better to be thought a fool than to open your mouth and remove all doubt." This is especially true for those of us who feel passionate about a topic and thus are compelled to say something. The question remains, when should we speak and when should we keep silent?

James gives us the "key" to answering this question in this verse. What this verse teaches is especially true if the topic makes you angry. Then you probably should not speak--at least while you are angry because you probably are not "self-controlled" or even more importantly, "Spirit-controlled." Angry talk just makes the one talking look like he/she's a nut or deranged. This past week a pop-star was quoted saying that they were so angry they were giving serious thought to blowing up the White house. This had to be rather disconcerting for the more than just a few people who work there! Apparently, the individual in question, noted for angry words and limited vocabulary, issued some kind of a restatement after being contacted by Federal officers who were a bit disquieted by the statement.

Thinking people "think" before they speak. However, am I saying that one should never speak if he/she feels or believes strongly? No - that's silly. Jesus spoke often when He was moved, especially when deeply moved. One such passage is found in Luke 13:34, "O *Jerusalem, Jerusalem, the city that kills the prophets and stone those sent to her! How often I wanted to gather your children together, just as a hen gathers her brood under her wings, and you would not have it*!" Obviously, our Lord has deep feelings behind these words. In this verse, we can also see His great love for children. So if you feel you have a fire in the belly and that the message is "shut up in my bones" (Jeremiah 20:9)--that, you must share or combust, well by all means, if you can do that and maintain your light that will shine before men and glorify your father, share it! If on the other hand, you are simply spewing anger, just know that people will see you not as a light in a dark day but rather a bomb that is always just a few seconds from blowing up. For the sake of those standing close to you, don't be a bomb, be a candle. Preferably vanilla!

A recent example of how this kind of thing can happen. Brooks Marlow who plays for the Astros "A" club (Lancaster Jet-hawks) apparently is in hot water because he tweeted a thought about ESPN analyst Jessica Mendoza. Apparently, Mr. Marlow was distracted by Jessica in the "play calling" of a major league playoff game. Afterwards, both he and the Astros issued an apology for what he "tweeted." Frankly, I hope this doesn't hurt Marlow too much because most of us fail once or twice with this kind of thing in the land of social media. Here's a lesson I especially had to learn in my 30's when social media was newer. Just because you think it, you don't need to write it. Just because you write it, you don't need to post it. Just because you post it doesn't mean you shouldn't from "time-to-time" delete it! Especially when we are passionate, we should take extra time to make sure that our passion isn't blinding us from the appropriateness, or inappropriateness of our words. As Ryan Holiday notes, "zealot is a nice way to say, 'crazy person.'" I'm not perfect at this, and we must all work at this, especially in the land of instant tweets, grams, posts, etc.

In the 1980's, psychotherapists taught and ran expensive workshops that promised that releasing anger was the goal. They offered scream, bataka bat, and pillow fight therapy weekend workshops. The idea was that, if you could vomit out all your anger, you would be "clean" inside. What they eventually learned was that this did the exact opposite. Instead, people learned to get angry faster, with greater intensity, and over longer durations of time. God says that a person who easily loses their temper is a fool and recommends self-control.

The Puritan Thomas Adams noted, "*That which a man spits against heaven, shall fall back on his own face.*"

Straight Ahead friends! JT

12

Male and Female I

So the LORD God caused a deep sleep to fall upon the man, and he slept; then He took one of his ribs, and closed up the flesh at that place. And the LORD God fashioned into a woman the rib which He had taken from the man, and brought her to the man." (Gen. 2:21-22)

In 1159, Peter Lombard (Bishop of Paris) noted, "Eve was not taken from the feet of Adam to be his slave, nor from his head to be his lord, but from his side to be his partner." In the sight of God, men and women, as part of God's image and creation, "are equal!" "*And God created man in His own image, in the image of God He created him; male and female He created them."* (Gen. 1:27).

Having said that, let's also notice equality doesn't mean men and women are indistinguishable. God intentionally created men and women different and with similar or complimentary roles--but not identical ones. Perhaps it's not an accident that only mothers give birth and that Apostles were men. It's actually theologically and practically dangerous to erase the God-given differences between men and women.

My concern is that our young men and women will especially pay the price for the unisex movement in society today. Galatians 3:28 explains spiritually and theologically that if we are equal because of creation, we are even more equal because of redemption. So, the implication of "sameness" means that women ought to be equal to men in pay, work, society, and also in the voting booth. Both men and women bear the image of God and can relate to God, make decisions, work, and both can and should rule over nature. The work of women as parents is just as important as that of the man.

Except for serving as a pastor who exercises theological leadership in the church, the function of the woman in the life of the church is to be equally open. According to Romans 16:1, Phoebe was a deaconess. The role of a woman is different, but just as important as that of men in the life of the church. Having said all of this, as a pastor, I would still caution Bible-believing and evangelical women to be careful in their connection with the women's rights movement as we know it in today's society. My concern is that the legitimate desire for rights that are consistent with God's Word and creation--including the right to vote, the right to make decisions for vocation, children, education, to not be sexually or otherwise harassed, etc.--have been hijacked and merged with so-called "rights" that violate God's Word.

Too much of the Women's Liberation world denies the Biblical boundaries of marriage. Genesis 2:24, Mark 10:7, combined with other texts explain that marriage is to be heterosexual, monogamous, and committed to the glory of Christ. This has no doubt been abused by some men twisting

Scripture's teaching on the leadership God gives husbands (Col. 3:18). However, the Scripture is clear; "a wife is to follow the leadership of her husband" (unless doing so violates God's Word or her conscience). Women's liberation especially hates this part of the Bible's message largely because many men have not understood that submission is not the same as obedience and have ignored that part of this same passage that commands the man to love his wife as Christ loved the Church—that does not allow him to step on her and demand obedience. Yes, Women's Liberation is wrong; however, do not lose sight of the reason it exists. It is easy to submit to a man who loves his wife as God commands. Women's Lib did not come into existence because of men like this. More often I find that Christian women would LOVE their husband to be in leadership in their family but the husband, like Adam, is not willing to step into that role.

Straight Ahead friends! JT

13

Male and Female II

"For Thou didst form my inward parts; Thou didst weave me in my mother's womb. I will give thanks to Thee, for I am fearfully and wonderfully made; wonderful are Thy works, and my soul knows it very well. My frame was not hidden from Thee, when I was made in secret, and skillfully wrought in the depths of the earth. Thine eyes have seen my unformed substance; and in Thy book they were all written, the days that were ordained for me, when as yet there was not one of them." (Ps. 139:14-16)

Women's lib preaches, "it's my body." Well, actually no, if you are a Christian, it's not your body. You are a temple and you and your body belong to God (1 Cor. 6:15).

The clearest violation of Women's liberation is the wholesale murder of the unborn. The belief that a woman can simply discard the life of another life inside her because it's "her body," demonstrates the twisted nature and selfishness of much of women's liberation. It's not liberation from men that is driving most of this. It's liberation from the God of the Bible and His authority. I would urge Christian women who feel compelled to stand up for legitimate rights to be very clear that you draw the same lines that Scripture does and guard your heart so you don't become "a Jezebel" in spirit or practice. Much of the Women's Liberation movement has its roots in anti-Christian Humanism, Darwinism, Atheism, and Postmodernism. This makes it very popular in our "modern" godless society and even in some corners of non-discerning evangelicalism.

Christian men play a part in a woman's willingness to submit. A woman I know told me that she will never forget hearing a man at a conference she attended who was sitting at the table behind her say, "Well, I listen to my wife and how she feels, but when push comes to shove, someone has to make the decision, so I get two votes and she gets one." She said that it took all the self-control she could muster not to tell him what she thought about his voting system!

She also told me that she will never forget the words of a dear pastor, Darryl Delhousaye when he was at Scottsdale Bible Church. Darryl taught that, in a marriage, the husband is to present the course he believes God is directing him to take as the leader of his family. The wife, hopefully prior to marriage, agrees to this plan. They enter the boat (marriage) and he takes the wheel and she the rudder. As long as he steers them in the agreed upon course of travel, as long as he is submitting to God--all is well. Her job, however, is to hold fast to the rudder should he start to turn the wheel in the wrong direction and stop submitting to God. Too many men forget that the only creation that was not good was man without. The woman was given to him to complete him because she has strengths he does not.

This same principle applies to submission within the Church. We are told to submit one-to-another (Eph. 5:21).

Leaders, through prayer, study, and God's guidance develop a plan. The plan, or "course" is then submitted to the Church. Each member then submits themselves willingly to join the leaders on this journey. The congregation then steps into the boat (the plan.) The leaders take the "wheel" and the congregation takes the "rudder." As long as the leadership steers in the direction of "the plan", continues to submit to God's plan, and stays on course, all is well. The role of the congregation is, should the leadership begin to steer in a direction against "the plan", to hold the rudder tight.

Straight Ahead, friends! JT

14

Don't Give Up

"Therefore, since we have so great a cloud of witnesses surrounding us, let us also lay aside every encumbrance, and the sin which so easily entangles us, and let us run with endurance the race that is set before us." (Heb. 12:1)

Don't give up! You don't understand the impact of your faith and determination. We all get tired. It's easy to be discouraged when you don't see tangible results or you don't see that others are making the same sacrificial "giving" as you do. It's also hard to keep on the path you believe God placed you on when loved-ones and even friends misread or struggle to understand why you do what you do. This is hard on a few levels.

It's hard because we all have an expectation that those who know us would (or should) trust that our motivations are honorable. When people second-guess our decision to serve God in a specific context, it is easy to begin to doubt the nature and strength of those relationships that are sometimes very important to us. One of the truths we miss when going through a hard season of life and ministry is that, frankly, we are surrounded by not only these great men and women of faith who have run faithfully before us (check out that list in Hebrews 11 and notice their hardships), but also people who today are making a difference in spite of great trials and opposition. If you are going to make a difference in the lives of others, it requires you to pay the price of leadership. Leadership is hard because that call demands that not only will you have to regularly climb the hill while enemies are throwing rocks, but you will by necessity and life-call be helping others up the same hill, watching sadly as many of them "quit the climb."

We read of the kind of opposition that Nehemiah faced in the midst of trying to rebuild the walls of Jerusalem. As you read in Nehemiah 6 of the accusations thrown towards Nehemiah and the lies of Sanballat, Tobiah, and company, it's interesting to note that Nehemiah gives his enemies an answer, but never takes his focus off the work of the hour. In Nehemiah's case, he had the spiritual aid of Ezra, who was working on the re-establishment of the spiritual walls of God's people, namely the Law. Just when you think you are all alone, God will bring another mud-covered soul who is also faithfully slogging up the same kind of hill, in his own corner of the Lord's vineyard. Enjoy those moments. Looking at the bigger picture, understand that they are also needed because it is not possible for you to meet all the needs in every area. You will need lots of help. Once in a while, God will give you a few moments to lean on each other, laugh, and enjoy the respite.

Scripture notes, in a variety of places, that we are in a battle. God needs His non-commissioned officers (whose names are not necessarily known on earth although in

Heaven and Hell they are known) to win the day. The privates (who are often strategically positioned on the battlefield) need you! The Generals (who are often tactically positioned far off from the battlefield) need you! You might think nobody sees. They see. Many secretly appreciate you. It probably is a reality that they won't fully appreciate you until you are on the other side. That's okay. You will have accomplished your mission and you will have mentored enough leaders to carry on in your absence. Many of you reading are already doing this and making a difference.

"Christ ceaseth not to work by His intercession with God for us, and by His Spirit in us for God, whereby He upholds His saints, their graces, their comforts in life, without which they would run to ruin." (William Gurnall)

Straight Ahead, my friends. JT

15

Thinking then Feeling

My biggest struggle is not with others. It's with me. That is likely the same for you. Proverbs 25:28 says, *"Like a city that is broken into and without walls is a man who has no control over his spirit."* Also consider 2 Cor. 10:5, *"We are destroying speculations and every lofty thing raised up against the knowledge of God, and we are taking every thought captive to the obedience of Christ."*

Perhaps one of the most important daily fights of faith is self-discipline over our emotions. My issue is "I'm a sap" and getting sappier by the second. I have several strikes against me. God has given me a love for people. That's great but if it's not held in check by my love for God and His Word, my love for people could kill my ability to deliver the tough news that my job often demands. A second strike against me is I quickly have an ability to feel the pain of others. If I'm not careful with that one, I can wrongly pick up the offense of others and sinfully make it my own. A third strike against me is that I'm very, very French! The French, as with all Latin-based people, can be very emotional. Need I say more? The result of my being a French-American sap is that, if I am not very vigilant, I can easily be controlled or hijacked by my emotions.

One of the dear leaders at my childhood church (who I have had great respect for over the years) is a former coach and high school mentor, Coach Buddy MacDonald. Coach "Mac" (affectionately named) said something a few years ago in a sermon he preached for a graduation I'll never forget. He explained to a full auditorium that the world today has this theory that one should always follow their heart. In a line that remains one of the top lines I've ever heard in a sermon, Buddy challenged us with, "Whatever you do, don't follow your heart!" I actually heard some people gasp. It was fantastic. The genius about Coach Mac's sermon is that, while it's not very Disney, it is Biblical! He quoted appropriately from Jeremiah 17. Your heart is pre-wired for wickedness and it is deceptive. This is another way of saying your emotions have been affected by the fall. They are still impacted by the remnants of our flesh and left-over depravity, and we must maintain a holy diligence to rule them (our emotions) instead of the other way around (Rom. 7:15-16). That is like the tail wagging the dog.

Over the years, I've explained that, especially when we are working through times of trial or transition, we especially need to keep our eye on the "John 13:17 principle." Jesus notes, *"If you know these things, you are blessed if you do them."*

Coming out of this are three powerful observations:

(1) Right thinking (if you "know right") encourages right action ("do right").

(2) When you "do right" that encourages right emotions ("happy").

(3) When you have healthy emotions, that encourages further right thinking.

All that has to happen is to lose your grip on right thinking to find yourself stuck in harmful thinking and easily hijacked by your emotions. Paul notes in Philippians 4:8, *"Finally, brethren, whatever things are true, whatever is honorable, whatever is right, whatever is pure, whatever is lovely, whatever is of good repute, if there is any excellence and if anything worthy of praise, let your mind dwell on these things."*

History is full of examples of what happens when our decision-making is based on heart first instead of head. Emotional based decision-making is often disastrous. Even if (and maybe especially if), it's dripping in a kind of pseudo-mystical-pietism. My dear theology mentor Dr. Rolland McCune used to say, "anything that bypasses the mind is dangerous!" "Christian Europe" waged a hundred and fifty year long war against Islam in the Middle East from 1096-1248 AD. History records their seven "crusades." There were notable victories. Godfrey's victory in Nicea, Antioch and Jerusalem. King Richard's exploits were almost "other worldly" defeating the Islamic armies at Acre, Joppa and even a treaty with Saladin himself! The combined losses were staggering. Especially egregious was the "children's crusade in 1212 A.D. Most of the children who marched off to war were either lost at sea, sold as slaves or otherwise quickly perished by disease or battle.

So back to our starting thought – we must think about what we think about. It is crucial that we bring every thought into the captivity of Christ (2 Cor. 10:5). May God give us grace to make sure the mind of Christ is our focus because our emotions are merely reflections of our thoughts. If I think "danger", my emotion will be fear or anxiety. If I think, "that was not right or fair", my emotions will be anger and disappointment. That is why God tells us to take our thoughts captive.

A friend of mine told me that one day she attended a service in which a man, dressed as Peter, quoted the entire book of I Peter. Afterwards, he gave his testimony. He stated that, years ago, he was completely and totally consumed by porn. His wife told him that she was done! God told him that he needed to take his thoughts captive, which means that he intentionally decides what will consume his thoughts. He began memorizing "books" of the Bible. Yes, books! Now, many years later, he was working on his eighth book, Hebrews, and gave this testimony. In memorization, he discovered that God is able to wash all the evil and disgusting pictures Satan had stored in his mind—out of his mind. So, every time he caught himself focusing on negative thoughts from the past or pictures that were imbedded in his brain, he worked on the chapter of the Bible he was focusing on that week. He stated that, as a result, all those negative memories and pornographic images eventually were all gone. His wife stood up and said that this man was a totally and completely different man than the one she was close to divorcing and verified that his testimony was true.

Straight Ahead, my friends! JT

16

Compassion in Grief

Here are two Old Testament passages that have meant much to me in the dark hours of the soul. I discovered these passages in my teen years. I hope they can also help you.

"For the Lord will not reject forever, for if He causes grief, then He will have compassion according to His abundant lovingkindness. For He does not afflict willingly, or grieve the sons of men." (Lam. 3:31-33 - This is one of Pastor Joel's favorite passages on grief.)

But now, thus says the LORD, your Creator, O Jacob, and He who formed you, O Israel, 'Do not fear, for I have redeemed you; I have called you by name, you are Mine! When you pass through the waters, I will be with you; and through the rivers, they will not overflow you. When you walk through the fire, you will not be scorched, nor will the flame burn you. For I am the LORD your God, the Holy One of Israel, your Savior; I have given Egypt as your ransom, Cush and Seba in your place. Since you are precious in My sight, since you are honored and I love you, I will give other men in your place and other peoples in exchange for your life. Do not fear, for I am with you; I will bring your offspring from the east, and gather you from the west.'" (Isaiah 43:1-5).

I understand the covenant and prophetic context of the Isaiah passage, but the implications for all of God's children are clear. God has compassion, but more important than that is the part you and I are to play in the completion of His plan and the pruning of His vineyard.

In consideration of the Isaiah passage, God explains that, even though Israel was not perfect, His unconditional favor towards Israel would allow for the punishment of three pagan nations (namely Egypt, Ethiopia, and Seba). God chose for them to receive the wrath and judgment that could have been Israel's. Egypt specifically had been a ransom or "covering" of Israel. Significant is the covering of the blood in the various festivals (such as "The Feast of Passover and Unleavened Bread) of Israel remembering God's deliverance. (Edward Young, *The Book of Isaiah*, Eerdmans Publishing, 3:143). Sometimes that means things happen we would not choose. Even when it doesn't make sense, God's way is always best.

One more: "…*Weeping may last for the night, but a shout of joy comes in the morning."* (Ps 30:5). Grief comes, but it is not our birthright as God's children. Joy is.

One way to work through grief is to remember that Jesus also experienced this emotion while He was here on earth. "In 1858 Scottish missionary John G. Paton and his wife sailed for the New Hebrides (now called Vanuatu). Three months after arriving on the island of Tanna, his wife died. One week later his infant son also died. Paton was plunged into sorrow. Feeling terribly alone, and surrounded by savage people who showed him no sympathy, he wrote, "Let those who have ever passed through any similar darkness as of midnight feel for me. As for all other, it would be more than vain to try to paint my sorrows...But for Jesus, and His fellowship...I would have gone mad and died." (Daily Bread, August 6, 1992. 1 Thessalonians 4:13).

The New Testament saint, in a similar way, is comforted with the thoughts of Romans 8:1, *"There is therefore now no condemnation..."* Jesus took our wrath. When it's dark for the believer, there is still light because He is the Light.

Straight Ahead friends! JT

17

Hard Dates

I have always loved Rom. 8:28. Here Paul notes, *"And we know that God causes all things to work together for good to those who love God, to those who are called according to His purpose."*

A central part of this verse is a reminder that God works out all the details of life and makes them "good" (in one way or another) for His children.

Alexandrina Victoria lived from May 24, 1819 until January 22, 1901. The Queen of the United Kingdom of Great Britain and Ireland lived a life that was, at times, "larger than life." Victoria married her first cousin, Prince Albert of Saxe-Cobury and Gotha in 1840. The royal couple had nine children, all of whom married into various royal families across Europe. Ironic that just a little over a decade after her death, her royal descendants were fighting each other in the first World War of the twentieth century. The notable tragedy of Victoria's life was the death of her beloved husband, Prince Albert in 1861. It's said that each year the queen would relive her love and loss of Albert by going into mourning leading up to the blasted date of December 14, 1861.

Some of us have hard dates on the calendar. I have three or four that are particularly hard because of a disappointing event that I had to walk through. Sometimes on those days my mind will rush back to these occasions and it's like I'm in the presence of an old enemy, a deep sorrow I can't describe, and I'm forced to run through something of a mental checklist and work through a variety of emotions. How should we think about these dates? As God's children, we can be helped on those days by specific comforts. God is still good! He is all-wise even when there are times we don't understand why that which we wanted to happen did not happen or why that which we did not want to happen, happened. Why did God allow this to plow right into the middle of our "happy life" and make the mess that it did? Or, why like Job, when I was trying to do right, did God allow precious gifts to be stolen from me like my health or that loved-one ripped from me? This is especially hard when we know at the conviction level that this wrong thing, this unjust thing, this unthinkable thing happened and it will never unhappen.

Ultimately, God is good and has a plan we can trust even when we don't understand. God sees the beginning from the end and we very much do not! We know that God will work it out even though, we like Habakkuk, find that our inward parts tremble (Hab. 3:16). He has a plan that includes turning ashes into beauty.

I think part of "faith" is loving and forgiving those who disappoint us even when they were/are clueless as to the hurt they caused. I've noticed some of us struggle with those who have passed because we didn't get to say everything we wished we could have said. Sometimes we were wounded by the choices of others. Even when that "choice" impacted us in a hard way. Even though we might want to take it personally, even when it might actually have been meant personally, love and forgiveness are the high road--always. I think it is an act of faith and even an exercise in worship--and Heaven takes notice. This is true especially when in our natural minds, it might never make sense, at least on this side of heaven. We must walk by faith.

All the dark, intricate, puzzling providences at which we were sometimes so offended... we shall [one day] see to be to us, as the difficult passage through the wilderness was to Israel, "the right way to the city of habitation" (John Flavel)

Straight Ahead my friends! JT

18

Running from Fools

Consider Proverbs 14:7-9, *"Leave the presence of a fool, or you will not discern words of knowledge. The wisdom of he prudent is to understand his way, but the folly of fools is deceit. Fools mock at sin, but among the upright there is good will."*

It's foolish to call someone "a fool." Actually, some people we might be tempted to call a fool, might simply be ignorant. They may be naive about some aspect of life, but that is not the same as them being a "fool."

Having said that, there will be times when we are clearly dealing with a fool because of the description God's Word gives about a fool. I've had to learn, even in ministry, to be careful not to give too much time to foolish people. I know of a leader who every time an individual left his ministry, got on the phone and called as many other leaders as he could to poison others against these ministry partners who had moved on. Years ago, every time I was with this person he wanted to talk about everyone who had failed him or everyone with whom he disagreed. Scripture warns us to run away from these kinds of people. Frankly it's probably better to spend time with a sinner who knows he's a sinner and wants to no longer be a sinner than to spend time with a fool. Fools are often overconfident and self-righteous. Here's God's warning. If you spend too much time with a fool, you can actually become foolish yourself! It's why Paul tells us in 1 Corinthians 15:33, *"Do not be deceived: 'Bad company corrupts good morals."*

Another way in which foolishness shows up in the realm of secular and ministry leadership is when you have an individual or individuals who refuse to work in consensus with other leaders in the same organization. It's not to say it's wrong for a leader to make a tough call when that's legitimate to his office. However, I've seen it up close and personal when two or three leaders are trying to control the direction of an organization and one and all are overstepping their legitimate role. A clear example from church history was the occurrence of three popes who all claimed papal authority, at the same time. In 1409 the Latin Pope, Gregory XII claimed status as *"Vicarious Filii Dei"* (Vicar of Christ, or more literally, "Representative of the Son of God."). At the same time, Pope Benedict XIII claimed the same status in Avingon, France. Not to be out-shown was Pope Alexander V demanding the right of Catholic ruler-ship by virtue of the Council of Pisa! While it's easy for evangelicals to point out the ridiculous nature of this kind of thing, there are constantly Protestant ministries that are pulled part from the inside out by the same kind of power-struggle in the name of Gospel virtue.

On May 2nd, 1878 Minnesota experienced a tragedy. Eighteen workers where killed when the Washburn, a flour mill near St. Anthony Falls not too far from Minneapolis, exploded. Apparently a starch-like flour, when existing in enough quantity and when floating around in the air (especially in powder form) is hit by an electric arc, the result can be catastrophic. Who knew? This can also happen with coal, magnesium, and other substances.

Here's the point: our relationships can be like flour, which, on its own, can be pizza! When mixed with a dangerous element, these same ingredients can become something like a bomb! Remember this the next time you are faced with the decision of maintaining a relationship that might not be obviously healthy for you. Will this relationship help you? Is your mix with this person potentially dangerous? David found out, by dodging a spear, that Saul had a foolish and explosive temper. *"...I will pin David to the wall..."* (1 Sam. 18:11). Fools can be harmful to your health!

Straight Ahead friends! JT

19

When Life is Hard

"Then Job arose and tore his robe and shaved his head, and he fell to the ground and worshiped. And he said, 'Naked I came from my mother's womb, and naked I shall return there. The LORD gave and the LORD has taken away. Blessed be the name of the LORD.'" (Job 1:20-21)

Have you ever had a bad day? How about a hard week, month, or year? Ever faced a difficult transition in your life? What is often true is that when we face these kinds of trials, making the ordeal about ten times harder than it needs to be, our propensity is to look over our shoulder and worry about what people must think of us. That is especially true of men, when we go through a hard transition, like a change in our job.

Did you know that the Bible is full of examples of God's men facing difficult times? Consider Joseph setting in jail in Genesis 39. Also notice that the "*LORD was with Joseph and showed him mercy* (while he was in jail!)." Consider that Moses was a fugitive from Egypt for 40 years after killing the

Egyptian. Consider John the Baptist sitting in Herod's jail in Matthew 11--soon to have his head cut off. Consider Peter in (and quickly out of) jail (Acts 12). Consider the pain of Peter when he caught himself denying Jesus (John 18:15-27). The Apostle Paul was in prison so much I'm convinced when this great man of God marched into town he was always looking for where the prison was because he knew, in a matter of days, he'd be there! Consider great men of God who clearly struggled with depression and/or anxiety. Men such as Abraham (Gen. 15), Jonah (chapter 4), Job (his book), Elijah (1 Ki. 19 (especially verse 4), Jeremiah (again, throughout his book), and of course David (Ps 6, 13, 25, 27, 31, 32, 34, 37-40, 42-43, 46, 51, 55, 62-63, 69, 71, 73, 77, 84, 86, 90-91, etc.).

Consider that God's own Son, our Lord and Savior Jesus of Nazareth, had a three year ministry and lived only thirty-three years on this planet. Remember at the beginning of those three years He was tempted in the wilderness for forty days during which He was hungry and was so spent afterwards in His humanity that angels needed to come and minister to Him. After three years of ministry, only a hundred plus followers met the Holy Spirit in the upper room. I Cor. 15:6 tells us, *"After that He appeared to more than five hundred brethren at one time..."* Imagine how God used the work of His Son after Jesus had died, rose, and ascended. After the Holy Spirit showed up in power, changing those same spineless Apostles into spiritually strong men who had backbones of steel. Jesus' family came to faith (after the resurrection) like James who would pastor the church in Jerusalem. These few followers of Christ were so changed they turned the world upside down (Acts 17:6)!

Here's the take home. You are not loved and you are not significant because of what you do (although what you do matters to others and Heaven). You are ultimately significant because of who you are "in Christ" and what you are "by Christ." When you face a transition, just remember that this doesn't make you a failure--even when part of the transition was opened up because you failed to some degree or another. Failure doesn't make you a failure, it makes you human. Too many of us put ourselves in this self-imposed prison of false guilt because we think we haven't been successful enough. Stop that! You're being faithful to your friends, your family, yourself, and your God. This is success! None of us are perfectly faithful, but God is pleased when we desire and walk in that direction.

Straight Ahead my friends! JT

20

Strength like Eagles

"Yet those who wait for the LORD will gain new strength; they will mount up with wings like eagles, they will run and not get tired, they will walk and not become weary." (Isaiah 40:31).

My father, who is just a few years away from his eighth decade of life, hikes in and out of the Grand Canyon every year. Dr. Jerry Tetreau serves as the Chancellor of International Baptist College and Seminary in Chandler, AZ. It was at this institution that I received two degrees and one wife! I've made the same trip with him seven or eight times over the years. We "Tetreau men" enjoy hiking and biking as we age. It's the only way we can recapture some of the athleticism we enjoyed as younger men. It's fun to listen to my father share about how God has given him a real platform of ministry coming out of the Canyon.

Dad loves languages, and so on a regular occasion he will be using his French, German, Hebrew, Latin, Turkish, Greek, Spanish, and who knows what else to communicate the Gospel and some life lesson to the fellow-canyon journeyman. Dad loves to show especially evolutionists the layers of the canyon as he questions the sanity of the theory of those massive geological formations being the results of ice formations cutting the canyon over millions of years. Dad will say, "I grew up on a farm. I know what stones that have been washed by water look like and they don't look like that!" I've actually heard dad explain that, as 2 Peter 2 explains, the Canyon is a testament of God's wrath and judgment. It's also a testament of God's deliverance. Almost every year, he has opportunity to share water, a little food, maybe a flashlight and a life-lesson with a hiker that was in trouble. When dad gets tired, he simply takes his time and continues forward, one step at a time. Eventually, he's out.

Often times, when we are overwhelmed with the challenges of life, it is because we are actually trying to solve the portions of our struggle that only God can solve in His time. So here is what I've started to do, when I catch myself trying to mentally figure out a certain portion of the struggle I'm working on in my mind, I try to identify the parts of the current situation I can and must be responsible for and then the parts that only God can change. My dear mentor in the faith and boyhood pastor, Dr. James Singleton, used to often quote Psalm 127:1. Here Solomon notes, *"Unless the LORD builds the house* ("Doc" would always stop here and remind the congregation that this is God's part)..."*They labor in vain who build it"* (He would continue with the reminder that this was "our part.") I'd encourage you to identify the parts of your struggle that only God can handle and then, in your daily prayers, explain to God that you understand this portion can only be solved by God in His time. If there is anything else you need to do, you're willing. In the mean time, you and I must be willing to wait on God.

It's been said that God will answer a prayer from his children with three answers. Sometimes God says "yes." Sometimes God says "no." Often God says, "wait." I think if most of us were honest this might be the hardest response from Heaven. We don't like to wait. For too many of us, we are tied emotionally to a certain task or event or something on the horizon. Until God delivers that event, we need to press on to other tasks that have been laid in our lap. When the time is right, we will be able to partake in the desired event. Until then, God expects us to be faithful dealing with the mundane. The normal. The routine. As you know, when God is ready to do His part, things happen. Think creation. Think Moses and Red Sea. Think Jesus and the Dead Sea. Think about the Resurrection of Jesus. Think of all those who were touched and healed by Jesus, just to name a few. More Scripture? *"Wait for the LORD; be strong, and let your heart take courage; yes, wait for the LORD."* (Ps. 27:14); *"It is good that he waits silently for the salvation of the LORD."* (Lam. 3:26). *"Therefore the LORD longs to be gracious to you, and therefore He waits on high to have compassion on you. For the LORD is a God of justice; how blessed are all those who long for Him."* (Isa. 30:18)

Straight Ahead my friends! JT

21

The Water of Life

"There came a woman of Samaria to draw water. Jesus said to her, 'Give me a drink'." (Jn. 4:7).

Jesus and His trek towards Galilee through Samaria in John 4 and specifically with His interaction with a woman at a well not too far from Shekem gives us a telescope into the heart of Christ for those who are lost.

At first glance, the Gospel reader might say, "So Jesus is asking water from a Samaritan woman: what's the big deal?" Well, culturally, spiritually, and practically this event paints an eternal mosaic of God's love for the un-religious, the unsaved, the wicked, and the culturally "different" from the typical child of God. The implications of this passage would fill a book. Actually, I've noted several dozen books written on this episode just over the last several decades.

To begin with, unlike Nicodemus who initiated a conversation about the needs of the soul, here we note how Jesus approached a woman who is spiritually oblivious and has no evidence of having a genuine heart for God. She is a harlot, to put it bluntly. At a key part of the discussion when this woman explains that she doesn't have a husband, Jesus pulls off the mask of the charade of external religion (i.e., the idea she is good with God because of her mountain). No she doesn't have a husband. She's had five husbands and the dude she is with now is another guy (not numbered with the five). This woman is at the well alone. It was custom for the women of the village to draw water together but that isn't happening here! No doubt in the minds of the neighboring women is the thought, "don't get too close to this gal, she'll steal your man!" She was shocked that a Jewish rabbi would talk to her and, on top of that, would drink with her. Jewish male spiritual leaders just don't do that. On top of that, they don't ever go to or hang out in Samaria!

This begs a question or two from us. Why the hatred of Judea for Samaria? Why had Judea become a nation of Jonahs towards Samaria? Why was the woman at the well surprised by Jesus' interaction with her?

As we noted, there was a gender divide (Jewish religious leaders never spoke with women in public--never). There was a racial divide (call it a blood feud that had existed for at least 500 years). There was a religious divide (we worship God on the right mountain while, "you people" worship God on the wrong mountain.) On a side note--those without a true heart of worship will always be fixated on whose or which external religion and practice is right. There was a regional divide. There was a tribal divide because Samaria was located essentially in the center of what was once the Northern Kingdom of ten tribes. From the time of Ezra and Nehemiah, the Judah-Benjamin Coalition of the Southern Kingdom looked down on, "big time", the Samaritan's mixture of false religion (their mountain) with Judaism. The point I leave you with here is to consider the last divide--namely a traditional divide. This is often the case with hatred from one group to another. The hatred is there in large part because it's always been there.

How especially out of place is it when Christian people foster a hatred for those who don't share our faith. We hate them because we've always hated them or we think of them as "those people." It goes off the chart when we can't even tell you why we hate or dislike them. We just always have. If that is our stance, we need the same living water this poor gal needed. When we are so dominated by hatred, we are lost and yet we don't even know we are lost. This indeed was the case with most in Judea who hated Samaria. They were under the delusion that God was pleased with their godless attitude towards the Samaritans. Jesus seeks to save the lost. Notice what the leading men of the village say to the woman after the visit of Jesus, "...*It is no longer because of what you said that we believe, for we have heard for ourselves and know that this One is indeed the Savior of the world.* (Jn. 4:42).

Straight Ahead friends! JT

22

Maturity in Speech

"Let no one look down on your youthfulness, but rather in speech, conduct, love, faith and purity, show yourself an example of those who believe." (1 Tim. 4:12).

This, of course, is consistent with a few chapters earlier when Paul tells Timothy to not allow leaders in the cadre of ministry leadership who are not "temperate" and "sober-minded" to look down on his youthfulness. Don't belong to a ministry or an organization where the leader has a pattern of being foolish with his speech. This is a serious matter. Proverbs 15:2, *"The tongue of the wise makes knowledge acceptable, but the mouth of fools spouts folly."* This is not to say that your leader has to be perfect--no one is perfect. All leaders will put their foot in their mouth from time to time. I've had to apologize for not being careful with my speech. All of us will speak before we think on occasion. However, the right kind of leader will have a clear pattern of being careful and gracious with his speech both in public and private.

A serious clue that you have the wrong kind of leader is when in public the leader is constantly saying the wrong kinds of things. This might include speech that is unkind or off-color. In an attempt to be funny, this is done at the expense of being serious. This isn't to say a leader can't be humorous--but not at the expense of being unkind or inappropriate. The right kind of leadership demands sober thinking and careful speaking.

A second characteristic of speech gone wrong is when the leader violates confidence over and over again. It is a serious breach of a leadership office when that which has been shared in private is loosely handled. It also demonstrates the leader really only cares about his own agenda more than the real heart-needs of those he leads. When he is careless with these kinds of confidences, he leaves the organization with which he is associated open to a lawsuit. A parishioner has the legal right to expect that his/her confidence shared with the pastor will be kept in the strictest confidence. If it is not, that parishioner has the right to sue the pastor and church if the revealing of that confidence causes that person harm. Even more, the parishioner also has the extended right of Privilege. This right and legally protected Privilege has been affirmed by several cases brought before the Supreme Court. The only exception to this law would be if there is a very clear and convincing evidence that a specific person, that this confession revealed, might also be in danger in the future. The same ethics that govern the confidentiality/privilege of an attorney, priest, psychologist, counselor, and social worker also applies to a pastor. It is therefore extremely important that those in these kind of leadership positions "guard their tongues"!

As noted in another devotional, those who love sheep will not be quick to blab the failures of God's children. Peter explains that the right kind of leader will have a love that, *"love covers a multitude of sins."* (1 Pet. 4:8). Titus (chapter two) explains that the right kind of speech from the right kind of leaders who want to shepherd God's flock must will be "sober-minded," "dignified," and "self-controlled"--just to name a few characteristics. This not only includes what we say--but also what we write.

Over the last 25 years of ministry, I've been involved in a variety of "civil wars" on ministry topics. I really regret a few of those battles. I should have been more restrained on a few of those occasions with what I wrote. It's not that I don't believe some of those topics were important. It is simply a fact that God has not called us to fight a war of words every time someone says something that we don't agree with. Solomon notes, *"The wise in heart will be called discerning, and sweetness of speech increases persuasiveness"* (Prov. 16:21). Publius, a Greek sage is noted for saying, "I have often regretted my speech, never my silence." How many of us have a reputation of not being careful with our speech.

"On a windswept hill in an English country churchyard stands a drab, gray slate tombstone. The quaint stone bears an epitaph not easily seen unless you stoop over and look closely. The faith etchings read: "Beneath this stone, a lump of clay, lies Arabella Young, who on the twenty-fourth of May, began to hold her tongue." (www.sermonillustrations.com). James 3 reminds those of us who lead and teach that we will answer for how we handle our authority and no doubt a significant part of that stewardship will include our speech, both public and private. This is a serious challenge for all of us.

Straight Ahead! JT

23

Facing Fear in Faith

"When I am afraid I will trust in you." (Ps. 56:3)

This verse reminds the believer that it's okay to be alarmed by the threats of life. That is normal. My personal view of the Biblical text that speaks about not having fear is that it is dealing with the kind of fear that goes beyond legitimate concern to a place of illegitimate control.

Consider Jesus speaking about this in Mt. 10:28 31, *"And do not fear those who kill the body but are unable to kill the soul; but rather fear Him who is able to destroy both soul and body in hell. Are not two sparrows sold for a cent? And yet not one of them will fall to the ground apart from your Father. But the very hairs on your head are all numbered. Therefore do not fear; you are of more value than many sparrows."*

Another passage that captures the teaching of Jesus on fear comes from the Sermon on the Mount. *"For this reason I say to you, do not be anxious for your life, as to what you shall eat, or what you shall drink; nor for your body, as to what you shall put on, is not life more than food, and the body than clothing? Look at the birds of the air, that they do not sow, neither do they reap, nor gather into barns, and yet your heavenly Father feeds them. Are you not worth much more than they? And which of you by being anxious can add a single cubit to his life's span?* (Mt. 6:25-27).

Jesus tells us the obvious here. We all will die, but don't be consumed about worrying about your death. The Apostle Paul and Peter met the end of their earthly ministry under Nero. The life and vineyard-work of Clement of Rome came to an end about the same time the Apostle John was exiled to Patmos under the Emperor Domitian. Trajan killed Ignatious. Marcus Aurelius executed Justin Martyr. Septimus Severus martyred Irenaeus. You get the point. The Church father Tertullian speaking of death noted, *"it is a poor thing to fear that which is inevitable."* (www.sermonillustrations.com). Interesting to note that unlike many of the other early church fathers, Tertullian lived to be an old man. An implication of the words of Jesus is simply this, you and I will not live one second longer on this planet than God has ordained. That's not to say we should not take advantage of medical care. It is to say that God has ordained the length of our days (Ps. 139:16). It also means we don't need to be overwhelmed by those challenges of life while we still have breath.

Something I've noted about the nature of crises. It is rarely as "end-of-the-worldish" as we first thought. Some like to quote, more-like misquote, Mark Twain as having said, "I've been through some really terrible, horrible, awful things in my life... and a few of them actually happened." Here Jesus clearly makes the case that being occupied with the thoughts of "worst-case-scenario" creates even more devastation and, further, "worst-case-scenarios" doesn't add height to a short man or days to a dying man. Courage then is not the loss of threat; it is the determination to not allow our illegitimate fears any relevance.

I think Heaven notices when God's children take a step in the direction of what they fear because that is against human nature. We want to run away. When we step into the winds of the storm, it's a partial demonstration of our trust in the Savior. The Father sees and is pleased by that kind of faith. 1 Peter 1:12 is an interesting passage to note. There the text explains that the angels are amazed when they see the faith of God's children who have not seen the Savior with their own eyes and yet take steps of courage despite that.

Matthew 6 reveals that God loves us more than birds and yet a sparrow cannot crash without Heaven's care and notice (Mt. 10:29). One of my favorite gospels songs from the past century found in many hymnals is *His Eye Is On the Sparrow*. So the next time you are weak and you take those steps of courage and think that no one sees, remember all of Heaven sees. You might say something like, "God, this bird is headed into that storm. I trust You!" If you listen closely, you can hear the words of Heaven, "well done thou good and faithful servant."

Straight Ahead friends! JT

24

God's Child is Unique

"For we are not bold to class or compare ourselves with some of those who commend themselves; but when they measure themselves by themselves, and compare themselves with themselves, they are without understanding. But we will not boast beyond our measure, but within the measure of the sphere which God apportioned to us as a measure, to reach even as far as you." (2 Cor. 10:12-13)

Paul explains in this passage that it is vanity and foolishness to compare ourselves to others. Here's the reality. What is it you have to excel in/at that gives you self-worth? Someone will always be better at that than you--always! The problem is not whether or not you are doing the best you can. The issue is that you're thinking that this ability, character trait, advantage, etc, somehow makes you superior or the lack thereof makes you inferior. You are delusional and at a disadvantage if you think your value is tied to being the smartest, wealthiest, strongest, or most whatever. This is one of the reasons Jeremiah notes, *"...Let not a wise man boast of his wisdom, and let not the mighty man boast of his might, let not a rich man boast of his riches; but let him who boasts, boast of this, that he understands and knows Me, that I am the LORD who exercises loving-kindness, justice, and righteousness on earth; for I delight in these things," declares the LORD."* (Jeremiah 9:23-24).

The reality is simple: each of us is unique and carries with us various results of God's design.

An example is my dear immediate family. My wife and I met at the Christian college here in Arizona we attended in our early twenties. After we married, she and I moved to the Mid-West to attend seminary and begin our many years of vocational service together. Along the way, God gave us three sons. God has designed the five of us similar in that all of us are wired towards ministry and leadership (that makes vacations interesting!) My beautiful and musical wife Toni (who mentored and encouraged our three sons who are also musically gifted and leadership-wired) has a style that is courageous. For her, life is clear and simple. If it's the right thing to do, you do it, no matter the cost. The apple, not rolling too far from that tree, landed square on the head of my middle son, Jeremy Austin, who also has a Herculean courage that dictates a life-commitment that is fierce. Jonathan Charles, my oldest son has a leadership style that is split between a mind that understands each member of the team has a job to do (and so he will encourage you to do it!) and has a very tender heart for those around him--unless you are lazy or refuse to tip! My youngest, Joshua James, is the life of the party. As a matter of fact, he is the party! He loves life, worship, and children. In a sense, he is the most expressive of all of us, to the fifth power. All of us are leaders, but our styles and strengths are different.

God has ordained diversity. No doubt there is a fun mix in your home, in your church, in your civic club, as this is true of the wider body of Christ. We all have strengths and weaknesses. *"For as the body is one and has many members, but all the members of that one body, being many, are one body so also is Christ. For by one Spirit we were all baptized into one body — whether Jews or Greeks, whether slaves or free — and have all been made to drink into one Spirit. For in fact the body is not one member but many." Don't compare...enjoy one another.* (1 Corinthians 12:12-14).

Straight Ahead friends! JT

25

The One Thing

Then in the midst of the assembly the Spirit of the LORD came upon Jahaziel...and He said, 'Listen, all Judah and the inhabitants of Jerusalem and King Jehoshaphat: thus says the LORD to you, 'Do not fear or be dismayed because of this great multitude, for the battle is not yours but God's. (2 Chron. 20:14-15)

God's children (in either the Old Testament era of Israel or the New Testament Church) are often concerned about "our enemies." The point is that God takes care of them. In 732 A.D., Frankish King Charles Martel ("the hammer") stopped the western invasion of Europe by Islam at the famous Battle of Tours. Martel's version of Christianity was hardly Biblical, yet God used his leadership and the armies he had assembled to protect Christians both then and for the last thirteen hundred years. Sometimes the enemies of God become "believers" in one way or another. On other occasions, God simply takes them out.

In 2 Kings 5, we read the account of Naaman, a captain (probably something like a general) from Syria. Naaman had taken into captivity a young Jewish girl to be a servant. When

Naaman contracted leprosy, the Jewish servant compassionately recommended to the captain that he contact a certain prophet (Elisha) in Israel. The hope was that Elisha might be able to help him by way of God's power. Eventually, the meeting happened and the rest of the story boils down to Naaman humbling himself to simply dip in the river Jordan. Despite his hesitation, he carried through and, sure enough, God healed the Syrian leader.

I do think there is an implication or even an application for God's children today. Many of us from time to time suffer from spiritual, physical, and/or emotional struggles. Those seasons are often very hard and very discouraging. When I have an opportunity to pray and visit with God's children who are going through that kind of season, I often will challenge them with this thought. You know you and I can't change everything, and sometimes nothing, about our circumstances. As a matter of fact, rarely are we totally in control of the challenge at hand. However, usually God has made it clear to us that there is at least one thing we could do to be faithful and even helpful to ourselves and those around us while we go through the present struggle. What is that one thing? Naaman didn't have to do a variety of things. God gave him one thing to do and when Naaman did that one thing, God accomplished far more than Naaman could alone.

I don't think it's really different for most of us. When we go through those tough seasons, let's seek God's face in prayer and meditation and ask the Lord to reveal what are the one or two things we can accomplish for God's Kingdom that will be a blessing not only to ourselves, but to others. I believe that often, if we will do this, God will show up and accomplish things we simply could not have accomplished or imagined on our own.

On some occasions, all we can do is pray. So, sometimes that's all we need to do, and God will do the rest.

I love the narrative we see in Acts 12 as Peter is freed from jail by angels. He didn't even think it was real at first! He thought is was a vision or something. Also, fun is the response of the brothers and sisters praying for Peter at Mary's house. When the dear servant Rhoda said, "Hey, Peter's at the door!", notice what this group says: "you're nuts." "Maybe it's his angel!" (Like that's not nuts?) "He's in jail and we're praying for him now!"

The point here is that often the best and most effective thing we can do is pray! You will notice at the end of the chapter an angel dispatches the present enemy of God's children Herod (no doubt the source of the fears of God's children). Herod is killed by the angel and eaten by worms. It's my guess that God used the same angel that busted Peter out of jail to kill wicked Herod. Apparently, God had it covered! Straight Ahead my friends...happy to meet you at the Jordan!

Straight Ahead friends! JT

26

Deny Yourself

"Then Jesus said to His disciples, If anyone desires to come after Me, let him deny himself, and take up his cross and follow Me"
(Mt. 16:24).

Tradition tells us that in October of 312 AD, a young Roman general named Constantine was marching against Rome to challenge Maxentius for the imperial seat of power when something happened to him. Some say he saw a sign in heaven like a cross and with it the inscription, "in this conquer." Not long thereafter Constantine claimed that in a dream Jesus appeared with two Greek letters – Chi and Rho. These are the first two letters of the word *"Christos."* His soldiers (after marching through a river and thus being "baptized") as a result, took this sign with them into battle, a battle that was won. Not long after, the "Edict of Milan" was given allowing Christianity, not only freedom, but political favor in the Roman Empire.

It's interesting to note that prior to this change, Christianity in Rome had been Biblical and even largely

"Apostolic" in contract with "religious" because persecution brought with it a holy purification to the faith. Once Christianity had been accepted and even politicized, the Christian faith of Rome began to undergo serious corruption in large part because there was no longer a cross to carry. To listen to not a few evangelical leaders, Jesus' problem was that He didn't understand Christian liberty. I've actually heard the idea that if Jesus is in you, you can do whatever you want as long as it's not one of the obvious "sins" (like murder). It's that kind of foolish "wisdom" that many have used who are now addicted to crack, porn, food, or you name it. (Jdg. 21:25). The point of the passage here is that if you are a "Christ follower", it means that you will become well acquainted with not doing what you want to do hence the word "deny." The problem with even a mature believer is that his/her sin nature/flesh is still very alive and well (even though it by way of position was crucified with Christ). As a result, he or she will enjoy (brace yourself) sin! (Rom. 7:21-23) So instead of shaking your backside at the body of Christ (like a spoiled brat) when you want to do something and the preponderance of believers for the last 2000 years have believed we should not do "that," perhaps we should consider carefully if our steps are prudent (I Cor. 6:12).

James 4:17 explains that if our conscience prohibits a thing, we should deny ourselves. Romans 13:1 explains that if the government prohibits a thing (unless it violates clear Scripture), we should deny ourselves. Jn. 3:19-21 explains that if something is dark or evil, we should deny ourselves. 1 Cor. 6:18 explains that if something is immoral, we should deny ourselves. 1 Tim. 6:10 explains that if a certain kind of pursuit of money will undermine our faith, we should deny ourselves. Mt. 5:16 explains that only by consistently living out "good works", will people see the light of our faith and glorify our Father. That doesn't happen unless we deny ourselves. 2 Cor. 5:17 explains that if we are a new person in Christ, our lifestyle should no longer reflect the old pagan ways. This means when those pagan opportunities avail themselves, we must deny ourselves. Romans 14 explains that if our actions undermine the faith of other believers, we must deny ourselves (even if that means passing up a juicy steak or some bacon--that's hard, I know!).

The problem with modern "self-centered" and "feelings-oriented" evangelism is that it largely misses the "deny yourself" part of the Gospel and the message preached is essentially "Jesus wants you happy, rich, and never sick." Please understand that this is a false version of Christianity. In the real version of Christianity, Jesus wants us to be holy. Happiness (or it's more robust cousin, "joy") follows later.

"Seek not great things for yourselves in this world, for if your garments be too long, they will make you stumble; and one's staff helps a man in his journey, when many in his hands at once hinders him." *(William Bridge)*

Straight Ahead friends! JT

27

Wise Leadership

"Then David said, "Is there still yet anyone of the house of Saul, that I may show him kindness for Jonathan's sake?" (2 Sam. 9:1).

You're kidding me! Right? In the ancient near eastern culture, you didn't do this!

In modern day culture, you also don't do this. Too often, new leadership in an organization (religious or secular) find it necessary to put down the previous leadership (person or team)...essentially saying they did nothing right and now saying that the new leadership is the courageous knight in shining armor who is here to save the day (I'm rolling my eyes). You have to know that puts off just about everyone who hears it. It demonstrates you are at best a rookie leader and at worst, a thoughtless or careless leader suffering from issues related to delusions of grandeur! First, they almost never were as bad as you make it out they were. Second, typically all kinds of people in the organization actually loved the previous leader. Third, no doubt the previous leader probably did a number of things better than you will! Even if there are certain struggles that the organization is going through because of past leadership failure, remember that eventually (if you make it long enough in your present position of leadership) under your management and leadership, the organization (or your wing of the organization) will have a wheel that falls off. You can then hope that the organization will think the best of you while you try to fix things. You can model graciousness best by being as positive as you can about previous leadership.

You don't have to lie about past failure, but you can choose on what you will focus. Leaders who try to come off as winners by putting down former leaders show off that really, they are the looser! The passage we started off with goes on to show that David demonstrates incredible kindness to the grandson of Saul (Mephibosheth). Of course, David, on more than one occasion, did not take the life of Saul, even when Saul was threatening his life, because David viewed Saul as "God's anointed," even when Saul was clearly twisted or deranged.

A common consideration or question for both secular and ministry leaders is, "when is it right to leave an organization?" Each leader/situation is unique, and a myriad of variables will impact each situation differently. Having said that "typically" a leader should stay in an organization when that organization is going through a difficult or significant change. Yes, there are bumps and potholes that must be navigated but in change there are always bumps and potholes. You as the trusted leader are needed because you are often the most tangible source of stability for others to hang onto in the midst of that change. Too many leaders leave just when their presence is most needed! You will always have critics. The visionary who wants to go in a fresh direction will always have detraction and resistance from those who are comfortable, petrified (or fossilized), and imbedded in the fabric of "what has always been." Typically, they should stay, and if they can't handle the new direction, they should leave! On the other hand, if the organization (as a whole) is not willing to follow your direction and renewed philosophy, often that's a sign that for your sake and the group's sake, it's probably time for you to move on.

Numbers 16 speaks to those lay-leaders in churches who try to undermine the leadership and direction of the pastors, elders, or deacons as a unit. The sons of Korah (of the Levitical tribe of Levi) just knew they had a better way than Moses and Aaron. Well, that didn't work out too well. God swallowed many of the extended family and consumed with fire the 250 men who supported the revolt of Korah. God spared some of the younger offspring of Korah, which eventually blessed Israel with the leadership of the prophet Samuel. To show that critics can sometimes change into that which is useful, the Korahites eventually became doorkeepers and custodians for the tabernacle. (1 Chr. 9:19-21). Another group joined King David and became accomplished warriors (1 Chr. 12:6). Another line became musicians and wrote various songs or "Psalms" that would be included in God's Word under inspiration (Ps. 42-50 and 72-85).

Straight Ahead friends! JT

28

Courageous Leadership

"And Eliab his oldest brother heard when he spoke to the men;
and Eliab's anger was aroused against David, and he said,
'Why did you come down here? And with whom have you left
those few sheep in the wilderness? I know your pride and the
insolence of your heart, for you have come down to see the battle.'
And David said, What have I done now? Is there not a cause?'
The he turned from him toward another and said the same
thing..." (I Sam. 17:28-30, NKJV)

David, when he was the "younger & the unknown David," on the eve of his battle with a 9+ foot giant was verbally "put down" by his elder brother Eliab about his presence at the battle. David in a great response (that has been repeated over the ages since) points out to his arrogant and patronizing elder sibling, "*Is there not a cause?*" David was a great and courageous leader in this moment (and many future moments) because he knew what it was to live for a cause that was greater than himself.

Here is a model of how the right kind of leader responds and performs. If you are going to live for causes greater than yourself, you will be stretched to your limits of strength and will face dangers, discouragements, discomforts, exhaustion, misunderstandings, and, in some cases, even your life and health may be threatened. However, if the cause is truly greater than yourself, it will be worth it! *"Now as they observed the confidence of Peter and John, and understood that they were uneducated and untrained men, they were marveling, and began to recognize them as having been with Jesus."* (Acts 4:13). The context here is Peter and John standing before the Sanhedrin with backbones of steel.

A quick devotional thought for Christ-followers. These men, especially Peter, had demonstrated weakness prior to this episode. What made the difference? These men had been with Jesus...before and after our Lord's death and resurrection. Courage is not found in the absence of fear or threat. Church history tells us that when the Roman governor asked the Church Father Polycarp to deny Christ so that his life could be spared, the godly Bishop, who had been a disciple of the Apostle John, responded, "Fourscore and six years have I served Him, and He has never done me injury; how then can I now blaspheme my King and Savior?" Frustrated by the faith of the Bishop the governor warned the Bishop that he could have him burned. Brave Polycarp warned the Roman about his appointment with the eternal fires of Hell." Polycarp was later martyred in Smyrna. When I read accounts like this, something jumps in my spirit!

There will always be frustrations and reasons for anxiety and disappointments. Courage is not simply the kind of thing which makes a soldier charge the enemy or a fire-fighter jump into a burning building to save lives. Courage is seen when a mother gives herself to her husband and children even when the husband and children don't understand the personal cost mom is making. Courage is seen when you determine to move on in life when you've been rejected by a loved-one. Courage is seen when a friend forgives the careless words or actions of another friend, even when the guilty friend doesn't know he/she's been offensive. Courage is seen when, even though no one says "thank you," a believer serves in a corner of the vineyard many believers don't even know exists. Courage is seen when you choose to live on, even in the presence of sickness, weakness, and discouragements. Courage is seen when you sing to God with joy in your heart, even when there are tears in your eyes. Where do you find that kind of courage?

One finds confidence and courage with the same person Peter and John found it--with the resurrected Christ. May God help us to see the reality of our resurrected Lord and the blessing which is ours to consider because we are raised in Him (Eph 2:6, Col 3:1, Rom 6:4). Courage is found there, in Him! "*Never will I leave you...I will never desert you, nor will I ever forsake you.* (Heb. 13:5).

Straight Ahead! JT

29

Real Love

"But Thou, O Lord, art a God merciful and gracious, slow to anger and abundant in lovingkindness and truth." (Ps. 86:15) *"Greater love has no one than this, that one lay down his life for his friends friends."* (Jn. 15:13).

We pastor-theologian types like to divide the characteristics of God into the "communicable" and the "incommunicable" attributes. The "communicable" traits are the kind of things that we can emulate as "image-bearers" of God. The incommunicable attributes are the ones that no matter how hard we try, we simply can't pull off. An example of the incommunicable ones would be God's omnipresence (Rom. 16:27, Heb. 4:13, 1 John 3:20). No matter how hard we try, we can only occupy one space at one time.

Perhaps one of the most precious shared attributes of the Trinity is the love of God. God is love (1 Jn. 4:8). Perhaps along with God's sovereignty and holiness, love might be one of the chief characteristics of the Godhead (that's a fun and deep discussion). Here's a thought I've had for some time:

how in the world can we "love" someone as God does and then, after that relationship goes sideways, we now "hate" that person? As a counselor, I'd say when this happens something is more twisted and wrong with us than it should be!

It's natural and normal for a relationship to change. Life is sometimes hard, and a common thing to happen is that a special relationship has to change because God has a wider plan and He moves us down the road of life. However, if you love someone that means, in many cases, you actually would be willing to lay down your life for that person (Jn. 15:13). How can it be that the molecular level of that emotion and commitment can so change that you now "hate?" From heaven's view, instead of being willing to give your life, you could take that person's life (Hate=Murder...check it out...1 John 3:15). If your "love" is now "hate," I have news for you...you, not the other person, have been poisoned and you need help!

A clear Biblical example is seen in 2 Samuel 13 when Amnon (a son of David) violated his half-sister Tamar. Afterwards we read that *"Then Amnon hated her with a very great hatred; for the hatred with which he hated her was greater than the love with which he had loved her. And Amnon said to her, 'Get up, go away!'"* (2 Sam. 13:15). Real love doesn't take, it gives. If real love isn't received, it continues to exist and does not change into hate. Real love is willing to live without, because love is about the other person, not you. So, I'm not suggesting you must let them back into your life at the same level as before the change/issue/event. What I am noting is that in many cases, it probably would be healthy to let them back in on some level. Even if it's good that the nature of that relationship changed, it's never good that you hate...period!

Hate kills. Love heals. It's why He shares this one with His children! Love so you can heal, my friends. It's God's choice and wise instruction!

Straight Ahead! JT

30

Battleship Strong

"For consider your calling, brethren, that there were not many wise according to the flesh, not many mighty, not many noble; but God has chosen the foolish things of the world to shame the wise, and God has chosen the weak things of the world to shame the things which are strong, and the base things of the world and the despised, God has chosen, the things that are not, that He might nullify the things that are, that no man should boast before God." (I Cor. 1:26-29).

In 1940, Germany unleashed one of its most formable battleships: the *Bismarck*. The fire-power and naval might of this vessel was unmatched in the Atlantic theater. The *Bismarck* (named after Chancellor and beloved national hero of the German people, Otto von Bismarck) would eventually be sunk in May of the 1941 in large part because of a torpedo that was launched from an outdated and slow biplane torpedo-bomber by the name of a *Fairey Swordfish*. As a fighting aircraft in the Second World War, the *Swordfish* was already considered obsolete at the beginning of hostilities.

British naval fliers called it "Stringbag." Well, one of the torpedoes launched from old "Stringbag" smashed the rudder of the behemoth German warship. The result of the blow was that the German battleship was forced into sailing in a large circle allowing the British Royal Navy to finish her off with several salvos from a fleet of capital ships from Her Majesty's Navy. What the *HMS Hood* could not do with all its fire power and British heritage, a slow British naval biplane was able to accomplish in one effective flight.

God made us in His image (Gen. 1:26-27). For those of us who are painfully aware that we aren't tall enough, smart enough, strong enough, sharp enough, good looking enough, or innocent enough, etc.--I have some good news. We don't have to be! All we as God's children must be is a vessel for God to use. When we respond in faith and submission to Jesus as Lord and Savior by way of salvation, He declares us righteous by way of justification and places us in His family by way of eternal adoption for usefulness and God's glory! Remember the words of the Apostle Paul, *"Where is the wise man? Where is the scribe? Where is the debater of this age? Has not God made foolish the wisdom of the world? For since in the wisdom of God the world thorough its wisdom did not come to know God, God was well-pleased through the foolishness of the message preached to save those who believe."* (1 Cor. 1:20-21).

To put an explanation-point next to this truth, God ordained that the four major women in the genealogy of Christ would paint the story of grace. Tamar was a harlot. Ruth was a gentile. Another was the wife of Uriah and an adulteress. The fourth was Rahab, another harlot. Consider God's use of Jacob (the deceiver). Note God's use of the Apostle Paul who, as Saul of Tarsus, had remained complicit during the stoning of Steven. Consider Moses who allowed his anger to cause him to become guilty of murder. Noah, after successfully saving the remnant of humanity in his construction of an Ark, eventually humiliates and defiles himself by way of drunkenness in front of his family. King David had Bathsheba. Abraham was willing, on two separate occasions, to have his wife pawned off as his sister to save his neck. Samson made a mockery of his vow, resulting in being blinded (in more than one way). Peter denied Christ and took His name in vain publicly, disconnecting himself from the Savior shortly after he swore that he would die for Him (and eventually did!) It's thought that the Apostle Paul was short and struggled with bad eye-sight (I can relate). The followers of Jesus were Galilean in a Jewish world where you really needed to typically *not* be Galilean to make it in the world of religious leadership.

Romans 5:5 reminds us that we have a secret weapon that more than levels the playing field. It's God's love. For to those of us who are God's children and by faith follow Jesus, God "pours" His love into our hearts through the Holy Spirit. The result of this is that when we allow God's work to penetrate our hearts, a powerful demonstration of God's light will then shine through us and thereby impact those who are hurting in a dark place (note 2 Cor. 4:6). So, the next time you come up against a task and you think you are doomed for failure because you don't have enough natural ability, remember that those who depend exclusively on their talent without opening up their heart "full throttle" will almost always fail. We, who lack this or that which the world would say are "must haves," have all we need when we open our hearts and throw ourselves head-long, dangerously, desperately, and totally to the task at hand. What we may not have naturally, we can surpass supernaturally because of faith in God coupled with conviction of soul, mind, and body. Remember God uses the foolish and the weak to lead the strong (1 Cor 1:27). How cool is that? Do you know what this means? It means most of the time when we fail, it is because we simply stopped too soon or are trying to accomplish the task in our own strength. Press on my friends.

Straight Ahead! JT

31

Sacrificial Leadership

"Finally, be strong in the Lord, and in the strength of His might." (Eph. 6:10).

Overwhelmed? I serve in the leadership of two ministries--as a pastor of a medium sized congregation and as a leader in a para-church ministry that takes me around the globe to encourage God's leaders in various corners of the Lord's vineyard. Believe me, the responsibilities of family, life, and ministry can often take me to a place where I get overwhelmed. I'm presently trying to finish a book or two on top of everything else I'm doing. So how do you get it done without going nuts?

First, who says it's always bad going nuts? Being nuts might make it better, so maybe you shouldn't worry about that part!

In all seriousness, because of your burn-out, it is easy to feel overwhelmed and feel like you're going nuts. Instead consider, that your burn-out might have a positive outcome if it causes you to think out of the box--because your stress has pushed you out of your current place of comfort and you can either give up or be forced to find another approach or way to think about the issue. Thinking out of the box often causes you to see things that were previously hidden.

There seems to be a clear pattern in Scripture. If you are going to be in leadership in the church or in a secular field, this will demand sacrifice. Jesus told His disciples that to serve in leadership in ministry, they were going to have to pick up their cross and follow Him. Leaders must give and typically they must be willing to sacrifice at a deep level. That does not mean that they cannot set boundaries on their time. It's never going to be fair in leadership. Most who don't make it in leadership don't make it because they aren't willing to pay the price of sacrifice that leadership demands or they have not set any boundaries and become so burned-out and overwhelmed that they cannot go forward. So, at times, being overwhelmed while doing what we can do to accomplish our mission is going to be part of the journey. It is not good if this becomes our "norm."

I think the Scriptures help us with a variety of wisdom points when we are overwhelmed. First, the Eph. 6:10 passage reminds us that we don't need to be strong in ourselves but rather *"…strong in the Lord, and in the strength of His might."* And we don't need to be strong by ourselves as Jethro advised Moses (Ex. 18:14-24). That's very good news for those of us who don't feel like we have all the strength we need to make it through the next fight, issue, deadline, etc. Second, remember that a wall is built one brick at a time. In Nehemiah, we see a leader of Israel back from the Babylonian exile leading an over-worked, under-protected group of Jews who, one brick at a time re-built the walls of Jerusalem in 52 days! It is interesting to note that a significant part of this wall overlooked the Kidron Valley--one of the toughest engineering parts of the wall.

At times, Nehemiah faced great opposition from within and without. He led the leaders with a tool in one hand and a weapon in the other. The steady discipline of Nehemiah's builders got it done. Implications for us? Make a list and do one thing. Take a break. Walk around. Call a friend. Look to heaven in prayer with one eye while keeping your focus on your task of the day (or the moment) with the other eye. Take a deep breath, do a second thing…repeat. Before you know it, the wall will be built. All of this really grows out of our knowing God. In knowing God, we then have the ability to "act" when it is of God that we "act."

Consider the following thought, "*We know not of the future, and cannot plan for it much. But we can hold our spirits and our bodies so pure and high, we may cherish such thoughts and such ideals, and dream such dreams of lofty purpose, that we can determine and know what manner of men we will be whenever the hour strikes that calls to noble action…No man becomes suddenly different from his habit and cherished thought.*" (Joshua L. Chamberlain, General Commander, 20th Maine, Union Forces, Battle of Gettysburg) Try it, friend.

Straight Ahead! JT

32

A Life of Grace

"And Naomi said to her two daughters-in-law, 'Go, return each of you to her mother's house. May the LORD deal kindly with you as you have dealt with the dead and with me.'" (Ruth 1:8)

Rich in grace are the words of Naomi to her daughters-in-law. Imagine the strength Naomi had to have to release these dear ones to go back to their own home country. Many who hold a view of theology will often speak of being committed to the Doctrines of Grace. Being committed to grace Biblically goes far beyond the Doctrine of Election. If you say you are committed to the message of grace, that ought to mean that, at some level, you are characterized by grace! It's sad to admit, but some Christians who fly a certain denominational or theological flag are some of the loudest arguments against that view.

Consider a few verses from the Old Testament - *"Evil plans are an abomination to the LORD, but pleasant words are pure."* (Prov. 15:26) *"The wise in heart will be called discerning, and sweetness of speech increases persuasiveness."* (Prov. 16:21) *"Pleasant words are a honeycomb, sweet to the soul and healing to the bones." (Prov. 16:24).*

It amazes me how God's children who talk much of grace and even to a degree believe much in grace are quick to dismiss grace when responding to those who have in the past or present missed the whole "grace" thing. Our twisted reasoning goes something like this because "they" (whoever "they" are) were or are "not gracious" and, therefore, we/you'll not be gracious either! Friends...this is the wrong call. We are not saying that this does not mean you avoid speaking truth. We are, however, suggesting that we speak truth "seasoned with grace" (Col. 4:6).

When we fail to speak truth with grace, the other party will typically respond in kind. It is possible that you might respond graciously and find that the other side will take advantage of what might be perceived as weakness. This is where faith is needed. Even though your name is "trashed", you respond by speaking peace towards them. In all honesty, I would rather not, especially when it's from a so-called "brother" or "friend" in the ministry. When this sort of thing happens, I'm wounded at a deep level and so my initial urge is too often not a gracious one. However, when we speak peace and grace even to those who would (or attempt to) twist and tarnish our reputations, we give God a chance to do something supernatural in our and their life when we respond in grace by faith. Here's a powerful thought: God has a habit of defending the reputations of His children who leave all of that in His hands. The reality is your character will defend you far better than anything you could say to your enemies or those who listen to your enemies. By the way, I have not mastered this discipline, but I want to. Well, may God give us all grace.

Straight Ahead friends! JT

33

The Acid Test

*"David therefore inquired of God for the child; and David
fasted and went and lay all night on the ground. And the elders
of his household stood beside him in order to raise him up from
the ground, but he was unwilling and would not eat food with
them. Then it happened on the seventh day that the child died.
And the servants of David were afraid to tell him that the child
was dead, for they said, 'Behold, while the child was still alive,
we spoke to him and he did not listen to our voice. How then
can we tell him that the child is dead, since he might do himself
harm!' But when David saw that his servants were whispering
together. David perceived that the child was dead; so David said
to his servants, 'Is the child dead?' And they said, 'He is dead.'
So David arose from the ground, washed, anointed himself, and
changed his clothes; and he came into the house of the LORD
and worshipped. Then he came to his own house, and when he
requested, they set food before him and he ate. Then his servants
said to him, 'What is this thing that you have done? While the
child was alive, you fasted and wept; but when the child died,
you arose and ate food.' And he said ,'While the child was still
alive, I fasted and wept'; for I said, 'Who knows, the LORD*

*may be gracious to me, that the child may live. But now he has
died; why should I fast? Can I bring him back again? I shall go
to him, but he will not return to me.'"* (2 Sam. 12: 16-23,
NASB)

David experienced the "acid test" with the loss of his
infant son. In the end, he came out with his faith intact.

It happens to all of us. That event that's frozen in time in
our minds. We can remember where we were. In most cases,
we can remember what we were doing. Certain sounds or
smells take us back in seconds. In my grandfather's
generation, it was where you were when you heard that Pearl
Harbor was bombed. In my parent's generation, it was where
you were when JFK was shot. In my generation it was
watching the space shuttle *Challenger* explode with a school
teacher inside. For my children's generation, it was that
moment you saw the planes fly into the World Trade Center.
For political junkies, it was that election you knew you had
sewed up only to discover a few hours later that the map was
too red or too blue to be true! On top of those events are the
details of our personal apocalypse(s). That air-squeezing, joy-
killing event when our universe came to a world crashing,
bone-rattling halt. Those events when "it" happened and our
lives changed forever.

For God's children, I call this "the acid test." For most of
us, we don't or can't talk about this one. It's too painful. It's
too raw. The acid test is simply this. As we are faced with the
ruins of that dream, we can hold the smashed pieces of it to
heaven and say that even though what happened should not
have happened, or because what should have happened did
not happen, I'm still willing to entrust that you are a good
God. (Hab. 3:17-18). It is tempting to think that if I had been

God, this would not have gone down this way. However, I'm not God!

In short, submission to Jesus of Nazareth even includes (and perhaps especially includes) the ongoing trusting of His wisdom for the parts of life we didn't plan. It usually means nodding in faith to heaven even for those wounds that are so deep that even you cannot put words to the pain you carry. That pain that is unimaginable. There is nothing wrong with asking "why, God" if that's followed with "what now, God?" God hasn't given us time machines, so we can go back and undo what was done or not done. Whether you like it or not, God allowed "that" to happen (or not happen) because He had a plan for you in mind. That part of your life, as hard as it has been, fit within the plan of God. The results of that, somehow combined with everything else God has done for you, gives you the "package" you need so you can carry out God's direction for you. That plan is what we call "your mission."

We all have a mission and they come in various forms. We must embrace all this means. It means (in part) that we are gifted with what we need to accomplish the tasks (which make up the mission) that God has placed before us. It also means that there might be some "resources" or "circumstances" we wish were different than what we've been handed. It helps not to sit around in pity and despair staring into space, mourning what isn't! God wants us to get off the floor, keep our eyes on Him, and plow every ounce of energy into being and doing what He wants from us. Yes, we've lost something, but what remains is enough.

Notice what you have, not what you don't! It doesn't take much. Yahweh had dirt, and so He made man. Yahweh had man, so He made woman. Israel had manna. Moses had a rod. David had a sling, five stones, and an ugly giant. Noah had faith, time, and wood. Gideon had a torch. Abraham had a promise. So do you if you are a believer in *Yeshua*! Joseph had dreams, some of them his own, some from Pharaoh, but all of them from God. Samson no longer had eyes, but he did have strength and a last opportunity to wipe out the hateful Philistines. Elisha had a second-hand cloak that had originally belonged to Elijah. Hannah had a son, whom she gave back to God. Jonah had a second chance! Nehemiah had rubble he was able to turn into a wall. John the Baptist had some locusts and wild honey. The widow had a coin. A "lepton" was worth about 6 minutes of a day's wage, but to God the worth of that gift had infinite value. Don't tell me what you don't have. All of us can make a list of what we don't have. What do you have? I don't know what you don't have, but I know one thing we all have. We have *now*. There is no guarantee that we will have later, but we do have it now. What will do with what you have? I leave you with a section of Scripture that describes a significant portion of my mission.

In Mark 9, John tells Jesus that he and others of the disciples saw a group of believers casting out demons in the name of Jesus. John continued to explain that because this group was not a part of their group, they told them to "stop it." Jesus rebuked John's thinking and explained that the team was much broader than their little group. This so much reminds me of today's ecclesiastical landscape. This group over here is fundamentalist. This group over there is evangelical. This group over here is dispensational. This group over here is Reformed. Too many leaders in their own little world have been self-deceived that only those that think exactly like them are greatest in the Kingdom. Heaven frankly will be a convergence of believers who while understanding the gospel correctly, only got it partially right with their particular denominational non-essential beliefs. It has always been the case in the body of Christ that too often we forget who the really enemy is. It is not the brother.

"Therefore, strengthen the hands that are weak and the knees that are feeble, and make straight paths for your feet, so that the limb which is lame may not be put out of joint, but rather be healed. Pursue peace with all men, and the sanctification without which no one will see the LORD...But you have come to Mount Zion and to the city of the living God, the heavenly Jerusalem, and to myriads of angels, to the general assembly and church of the first-born who are enrolled in heaven, and to God, the judge of all, and to the spirits of righteous men made perfect, and to Jesus, the mediator of a new covenant, and to the sprinkled blood, which speaks better than the blood of Abel."
(Heb. 12:12-14, 22-24).

Straight Ahead friends! JT

34

God's Plan for You

"For I know the plans I have for you, declares the LORD, plans for welfare and not for calamity to give you a future and a hope." (Jer. 29:11).

All of us can remember a time in our life when we were discouraged. The context of this passage is specific. So, if you read the verses before and after, you will find out that this passage is about God's promise to restore His people after the exile. I think it also has some clear implications even beyond the prophetic context in which it is found. God reveals His heart for His children in this Old Testament passage. As a general rule, if you as a believer are "here," it is because, as God's son or daughter, God has a plan to use you in a specific way to build Christ's Church and His Kingdom. He wants you to make a major difference in the lives of those with which God has placed you—and that's why you are "here." The result of this is multifaceted.

First, it means that if you still are breathing, you have a purpose and the ability to contribute to God's family. Over the years I've met numbers of God's children that think they can no longer contribute anything worthwhile. I've especially had dear senior saints say, "I don't know why I'm still here." Usually I smile and say, "I do!" I need you in my life!

Second, because of God's plan for you and because of the effects of regeneration and the new birth, God is for you and God's people who have the mind of Christ are also for you! So why in the world would you spend as much time trying to please people who are not for you? Too many of you allow people who say they are your friends or family to use past failures in your life to lock you up in a jail made by them and allowed by you. God is working in your life to give you a new chapter and then you allow some friend (so-called) or acquaintance who isn't for you to define who you are based on past failures--and you let them get away with that!

Third, because God has a plan that we can depend on, it means that we can work hard and not get discouraged when, from our point of view, God interrupts our plans and gives us what we think is a detour. It is only a detour from our plan--not God's plan.

Fourth, because God's plan is complete, it means that when it's our time to move from this world to the next, that we can trust the details because this too is part of His plan.

Here is a great illustration about the implication of our lives and the sovereignty of God as told by a writer in Our Daily Bread: *"In 'Our Daily Bread,' I told how a Christian providentially escaped death. An unexpected delay in New York kept him from catching Flight 191 in Chicago, which crashed with all 254 aboard. That article brought this note from a reader: 'I just had to let you know about one of God's great saints who ran to make Flight 191--and made it!' His name was Edwards E. Elliott, beloved pastor of the Garden Grove Orthodox Presbyterian Church in California. His plane from Pennsylvania was late, and a friend who had accompanied him to Chicago said he last saw him 'dashing forward' in the terminal to make his connection. As I read about Pastor Elliott's fruitful ministry, the question I raised in that June devotional challenged me with new urgency: 'Was Divine providence operating only in New York and not in Chicago?' Immediately the words of my correspondent came alive: 'At the time, Reverend Elliott didn't know he was indeed running to Heaven...' Mrs. Elliott and her four married children comforted the entire church. Their Christian faith and testimony in sorrow was most extraordinary."* (D.J.D., Our Daily Bread, June, 1980).

Straight Ahead friends! JT

35

Giving God your Reputation

"...and keep a good conscience so that in the thing in which you are slandered, those who revile your good behavior in Christ may be put to shame." (I Pet. 3:16).

Being of French blood, the author knows a thing or two about French history. No self-respecting Frenchman is unaware of the stories concerning Joan of Arc! A few years ago, I and my dear friend and ministry colleague David Deets (who wrote the forward of this book) stood at several monuments and a Cathedral connected to, "the Heroine of Orleans." In 1455 – 1456 AD, Pope Calixtus III allowed the mother of Joan d'Arc the opportunity to have the merits of her innocence re-tried after her death at the hands of the English and French rebels that had executed Joan publicly in the market square of Reims. This posthumous re-trial took place in the Cathedral of Notre Dame. A part of the re-trial was an in-depth look at the court records from the first trial in 1431 AD. After a lengthy discussion, the court's finding was that Joan was indeed innocent of the bogus charges that had led to her execution. The first trial had clearly been rigged the whole time. The court also found that those who had been involved in the original trial were to be damned as heretics themselves. Humanly speaking, it was Joan and her teenage courage that lead to the freedom of the town of Orleans and eventually the crowning of Charles in the Cathedral in Reims.[3]

"Keep your behavior excellent among the Gentiles, so that in the thing in which they slander you as evildoers, they may on account of your good deeds, as they observe them, glorify God in the day of visitation" (I Pet. 2:12). How do you respond to being slandered? To be honest, slander is one of the hardest hits I've had to live with in the ministry. It's hard because typically you can't say a thing. These twisted individuals take the facts and so tilt them on their head that anyone with a sinful propensity to gossip will eat the facts up like yesterday's left over "angel food" cake! One of the internal realities of leadership (ministry, secular, etc...) is that, if you are in leadership, you are a target regardless if you want to be or not. Those that follow have a mixture of fair and unfair expectations of you. In their sinfulness combined with your own, the result is often slander, gossip, and all things "tongue-poison." (Jas. 3:5-10) So how should we handle that?

The above passage in 1 Peter assumes you simply are going to face these episodes. So knowing that it's coming, this passage explains that the best defense is a godly offense. Namely, walking with God in such a way that reasonable people will see through the accusations falsely and wrongly made. The Scriptures remind us that we don't always need to speak out for our own defense. As a matter of fact, one

---

3 "50 Decisions that Changed The World" (*History Revealed* - Christmas 2017 Edition.)

Proverb expresses that you are better off just ignoring the spewing of the fool. Christ did not answer all His accusers.

A great passage in Scripture that gives us perspective is Daniel 6:13, *"...Daniel, who is one of the exiles from Judah, pays no attention to you, O king, or to the injunction which you signed, but keeps making his petition three times a day."* So, Daniel was targeted clearly. The rest of the story is one of the first "Bible Stories" many of us were privileged to learn on our parent's knee. What the story often doesn't focus on is how Daniel defended himself. He didn't. He simply allowed God to decide what was known or not known. In the end, Daniel is promoted and the schemers are eaten!

After decades of ministry, I've learned that the best way to respond when under attack is to say as little as possible and allow your true friends and your character to defend your actions and motives. That is especially true when the attack goes nuclear. In this regard, I'm thinking and praying for dear leaders who I have served over the years across the nation and even around the globe. Several of them are facing a season of slander. I am also praying for some ministries that are going through some days of challenge. I am praying that God will grant them strength in the days ahead. For those leaders who are facing times of challenge, remember that God will take care of your reputation: you don't need to worry about that. Far more important than what people think of us is what God knows of us. All we can do is devote serious time and dedication to our Lord, God's Word, and the dear ones heaven has placed in our life. Our character will win the day in the end, nothing the naysayers can say will ultimately derail what God is doing or what He will do. Stay the Course.

Straight Ahead friends! JT

36

The Foolishness of Atheism

"...The fool says in his heart, 'There is no God...'" (Ps. 14:1)

Atheism has been around since early man rejected the God of the Bible. A few years ago, Al Mohler wrote a fantastic book on New Atheism. In part, the book answers the question, how do we respond to the likes of Richard Dawkins, Daniel Dennett, Sam Harris, and Christopher Hitchens?

I will admit that while in general I have great compassion for those who are lost, it is often a struggle to have much compassion for atheists. As a side note, my personal theory is that many atheists have crossed the line of what the Gospels call, "the unpardonable sin," that only God sees. The Scriptures teach us that those who shake their fists in the face of God, in totality and with a final sense of rejection, eventually will experience God's final rejection. The result is that the Holy Spirit never again convicts that sinner of his guilt and he or she is left to walk their own way in life right over the cliff into the waiting arms of Hell and the damned.

In the Gospels, this sin was manifested by the God-haters who accused Jesus of being empowered by Satan. This is called in the Gospel, "blasphemy of the Holy Spirit" in Mt. 12:31-32. We see a similar thing prior to the flood recorded in Genesis 6:3, *"My spirit shall not strive with man forever..."* At various times throughout redemptive history, we see God removing his conviction and allowing man to run to his own eternal destruction.

Results of an anti-God disposition can be seen throughout the years. We can't really be that surprised when many of nonbelievers will do all they can to take Christ out of Christmas, schools, government, businesses, and life in general. Of course, they want us to substitute "Happy Holidays" for "Merry Christmas." "Merry Christmas" is essentially short hand for the old common greeting in past eras heard on Christmas day in Christian nations--namely, "Christ is born!" To the atheists, I say, I'm not moved neither am I surprised that you in your committed foolishness want to pollute Christmas. I can promise you I won't be celebrating the birthday of Richard Dawkins any time soon! You and Richard and every other atheist are fools, not because I call you that --no, you are fools because God calls you a fool. The good news is you don't have to remain foolish. Paul notes in 1 Cor. 3:19-20, *"For the wisdom of this world is foolishness before God. with God, For it is written, "He is the One who catches the wise in their craftiness"* and again *'The LORD knows the reasonings of the wise that they are useless."*

Romans explains that knowledge of the existence of God is self-evident and that no matter how hard you insist that God does not exist, in your conscience you know that's a lie. Romans 1:18-19, *"For the wrath of God is revealed from heaven against all ungodliness and unrighteousness of men, who suppress the truth in unrighteousness, because that which is known about God is evident within them; for God made it evident to them."*

So, you can receive heaven's adoption and heaven's wisdom by turning from sin to Jesus of Nazareth who took on flesh through the incarnation and was righteous by fulfilling God's law perfectly. He suffered so that your sins could be forgiven. As a result, you can be declared clean and forgiven with the righteousness of Jesus.

If you don't know God, perhaps a good start is just simply to pray to God and let Him know you desire to know Him. He will note this and listen to that kind of a prayer. Psalm 14:2, *"The LORD has looked down from heaven upon the sons of men, to see if there are any who understand, who seek after God."*

Straight Ahead friends! JT

37

Why so much Drama?

"Beloved, do not be surprised at the fiery ordeal among you, which comes upon you for your testing, as though some strange thing were happening to you; but to the degree that you share the sufferings of Christ, keep on rejoicing; so that also at the revelation of His glory, you may rejoice with exultation." (I Pet. 4:12-13)

How do you keep rolling when life gives you a flat tire? Nearly a decade ago, I preached a sermon from Acts 14 entitled, "Lied about, stoned, and left for dead!" That sermon was a blessing to a dear brother who had not long before been unfairly targeted by the vicious rumors of an individual in his life. Without preaching the whole sermon, a key principle is found in verse 20, *"But while the disciples stood around him, he arose and entered the city. And the next day he went away with Barnabas to Derbe."* You will notice that not unlike the Gospel lesson of the Good Samaritan in Luke 10, God used "dear-ones" in Paul's life to help him in recovery and ministry. One of the things I pointed out in that sermon was the role of certain Jews played who came from Antioch and Iconium. These individuals came specifically to Lystra to stir up opposition. My thought on that has always been "life already has enough drama!"

Why are some people just intent on stirring up more drama? Well, some people just are. You will notice their intent was to kill Paul. God spared his life (again.) Extremely instructive is the point that the next day, after a well-deserved evening of rest, Paul and Barnabas moved on down the road to continue their work. They didn't quit. Important to understanding this story is to note that Paul was with Barnabas ("the encourager"). Paul was with the guy with whom Paul he needed. Barnabas was gifted and called to the ministry of encouragement. I've noted that those who have been given more of a prophetic ministry almost always need a guy like Barnabas who has been called to come alongside and bind up the wounds of the one whose mouth is just a tad bigger. I have a friend who often finds himself on the pointy ends of conversation because he dares to go where lions dare not go. I often find myself saying, "Well what 'so-in-so' really means is this or that..." We need Pauls! Pauls typically need a Barnabas.

"I am the true vine, and My Father is the vine-dresser." (Jn. 15:1) In the verses that follow John 15:1, Jesus warns us that in order to make us more fruitful, He will allow us to go through seasons during which He will "prune" us. After watching God work in the lives of His children, especially His leaders, I have a theory. Here it is. Throughout our lives God allows a major wheel to fall off in large part because He is changing us into His image. This is true in our work life, in significant relationships, in our church life, and perhaps in relationship to our health. I see this so often that I don't

think there is anything you or I can do to miss the appointment for the "wheel change." It's coming and unless you plan to just live in a hole somewhere (that's probably where you'll discover that all four wheels have fallen off), you and I need to prepare ourselves to walk with God in faith through these pruning seasons He allows or invites us to experience.

In his excellent book *The Search for Significance*, Robert S. McGee explains that most of us will struggle in these seasons with one of four internal struggles: 1) The fear of failure (the performance trap)—This fear drives us to either perfectionism or manipulation of others (like spouse or children) to live up to your own or to the expectations of others. These expectations are often not even close to healthy or fair. 2) The fear of rejection (the approval addict)—This causes an unhealthy pattern of pleasing others at any cost as well as other, even more unhealthy issues. 3) The fear of punishment (the blame game)—Someone needs to go to Hell because certainly we all deserve it but you really deserve it because you aren't perfect! 4) Feelings of shame. This is a continual sense of guilt, loneliness, hopelessness, and inferiority. All of these are fueled because you are thinking logically and religiously, but not theologically. You don't understand who you are in Christ! You are loved, my friend!

Straight Ahead! JT

38

The Wrong Enemy

*"Jesus answered, 'The foremost is, Hear, O Israel! The LORD
our God is one LORD; and you shall love the LORD your
God with all your heart, with all your soul, with all your mind,
and with all your strength.' The second, like it is this, 'You
shall love your neighbor as yourself.' There is no other
commandment greater than these."* (Mark 12:29-31).

To this day, if you go to the northern region of
Minnesota, you will find an area called "the Iron Range."
This mountain range is found in the land of countless lakes
and soul-hearty mosquitoes. It is rich in heritage. Part of this
heritage includes an interesting mixture of mining, logging
and surprisingly "American communism."

Before I moved to Minnesota to pastor and work on my
postgraduate study, I knew about the Germans and the
Scandinavians. What I did not know was that, mixed into the
fabric of the Iron Range, there is a long history, going back
generations, of a real and ongoing hatred between American-
born Americans against Scandinavian-born Americans (such

as the Finnish groups). The same kind of extreme hatred was seen between Americans with Serbian background against Americans with a Bosnian backgrounds (and visa versa).

That's right. The same groups that tried to wipe each other off the map under the nose of the UN at the end of twentieth century and the same Baltic neighbors whose blood feud sparked World War I is the same group that in too many cases still hate each other today in the northern woods of Minnesota! These are only a very few of the many examples of "group hatred" that defy sanity.

Real animosity existed for a century (and more) between certain folk in the south for those "(expletive) Yankees." The Apostle John explains to us in 1 John 4:19-20, that if we say we love God and hate our brother, we don't love God as we should.

A farmer had prepared for months to win the state fair competition for "largest pumpkin" award. He had been diligent about every step of the pumpkin process only to have his prize destroyed by a particular rat on the eve of the fair. Enraged, the farmer spent the next day killing rats. He was so upset, he skipped the fair and spent the day sulking. The day after the pumpkin award was given out, he noted in the newspaper the weight of the champion pumpkin. To his dismay he realized he actually had several pumpkins that would have won even though his prize pumpkin had been destroyed by that dirty rat. He was so consumed by his hatred of the rat that he lost a competition he could have easily won. A lot of God's children remind me of that farmer. Are you so consumed with that rat from ten, twenty, thirty years ago that you have nothing left for a positive impact in your present life today?

This individual you hate is holding you prisoner to a past that cannot be changed. Do you even know why you are still feeling hate? Many times, we hold onto ill feelings for people for no other reasons than that we've always disliked them. Consider this, even if you had a legitimate reason to be hurt by "so-and-so", if your life has moved on and that person is no longer a real daily issue, why don't you forgive them and set yourself free from hatred's self-imposed prison? There will always be rats in life. It makes no sense to hold onto hatred especially when the reason for your dislike of that person really has no bearing on your present life. The Apostle Paul reminds us in Ephesians 4:31 that we need to get rid of bitterness, rage and anger. Let go of the rats! There are better uses for your hands.

Straight Ahead friends! JT

39

The Years of Locust

I love Joel 2:25, "*Then I will make up to you for the years that the swarming locust has eaten, the creeping locust, the stripping locust, and the gnawing locust, My great army which I sent among you.*"

This verse is loaded. I will simply say that I see a principle coming out of the context and meaning, namely that God is able to make up for the "time of locusts" in our life. This means several things. Perhaps one of the obvious realities is that He can make up for the time in our life when our life was fruitless. God can do this in the physical sphere of our life, as well as the spiritual.

I have a friend who just knew when the ".com" industry crashed that he would not be able to retire on time. This same friend again just knew that he would not be able to retire when the housing market crashed creating the "great recession." Guess what? He recently retired on time. God's math and laws of physical and spiritual provision rarely follows man's understanding of the logic and laws of the universe. Most of us have had those seasons in our life when we were at best confused. The best laid plans of mice and men were scattered right in front of our eyes and we just knew it meant disaster.

Maybe we were trying to figure it out and even as God's children, perhaps we made a mess of some things and one of those proverbial wheels fell off. How should we respond when it feels like all hope is lost? How can we process moving forward in life after a colossal failure? First, it's okay that there is a time in your life you really can't entirely wrap your mind around. It's like we say "what was that!" A tendency we need to avoid is spending too much energy and time thinking about past failures and seasons of being lost. The truth might be that God was taking you on a detour. It is these kind of detours that can keep us humble, build character, and mature us into the image of His Son. (2 Cor. 12:8-9). It isn't "all good," but God knows how to turn those kinds of things into good. As a matter of fact, He specializes in that! (see Rom. 8:28). Second, remember that God and "loved-ones" do not define you by the confusion of that season in your life. Only your enemies will, and they don't matter because they don't have your best interests at heart.

Third, there may be a time when the healthiest thing you can do for yourself is to stay away from people or places that take you back to that point in your life inhabited by the grasshoppers. It doesn't matter if you end up on your mission later in life, God can still use you in a mighty way.

Jerry Millner was an Irish shooter who represented Great Britain and Ireland by winning his first gold medal in the 1908 Summer Olympics. At the time of his notable victory, he was 61 years and 4 days old, making him one of the oldest gold medalists ever. In 1912, Oscar Swahn won this same gold medal at 64 years and 280 days old. Eight years later, he became the oldest silver medalist in this event at 72 years and

280 days old. In God's economy, it matters more that you show up as opposed to when you show up. Moses was about 80 when he led the Jewish people out of Egypt. Caleb was about 80 when he fought and took possession of his mountain! Jesus lived 30 years in preparation for a ministry that lasted only three years. The Prophetess Anna (in Lk. 2:36-38) was either 84 or 104 years young (depending on how you understand the math in this passage). She had lived faithfully, sharing hope concerning the coming Messiah, and, in the last chapter of her life, she gives the most important message concerning the Christ-child. As long as you live, you can serve God with the gifts and passions He's given you!

Straight Ahead! JT

40

Marital Oxygen

Ephesians 5:33, "*Nevertheless let each individual among you also love his own wife even as himself; and let the wife see to it that she respect her husband.*" *Song of Solomon 2:16, "My beloved is mine, and I am his.*"

My wife bought a sign with this phrase from the passage we just looked at and has it hanging over our bed! How cool is that?

Sadly, it's not possible to sum up every failed marriage in one phrase. However, so often the reason why marriages die is because the relationship stopped breathing! Without oxygen, all of creation dies, including and especially relationships. See what happens if you try to light a match in the vacuum of space! In a God-honoring marriage, both spouses take on the form of a servant. A marriage is a happy marriage when both partners are focused on serving the needs of their life-mate. Someone has rightly said that in today's society, you marry the person you love. However, in the Biblical mindset, we love the person we marry. The difference is significant and obvious. When feelings are more important than the decision, the decision becomes less important.

The result of that is a growing divorce rate that has even captured modern Christian marriages. One way to make sure your marriage doesn't end up broken is to make sure it doesn't start off broken. If you are willing to date someone who is primarily selfish, marriage is not going to be the magic carpet to change their character. Having said that, even if you marry a selfless partner, every marriage will have seasons of struggle to one degree or another. Successful marriages will, however, overcome those times of struggle by way of commitment to God and each other. A great example of marriage commitment is seen in 1 Sam. 1:8: "...*Hannah, why do you weep and why do you not eat and why is your heart sad? Am I not better to you than ten sons?*" Elkanah had two wives. Even though Hannah had a "womb that was closed," her husband loved her. This is Hannah's husband demonstrating selflessness and a total love commitment to his wife who at the time looked as if she could bear no children. The rest of the story is glorious. God blesses the two of them with children, the first of whom, Samuel, serves the nation as its spiritual leader.

When marriages continue to struggle, it is almost always because there is a loss of intimacy on the part of one or both parties. By intimacy, I'm not simply talking about the loss of a physical relationship, but I'm including the sense of "togetherness," "rapport," "friendship," and "affection." If intimacy is not present in your marriage, it is often because you or your spouse either killed it through bitterness or you let it die through neglect. Genesis 22:24 and then again in Mark 10:6-9, we are reminded that God's expectation for marriage is for us to leave father and mother and become united as one. In other words, we are to "grow in our union." So many Christians have fooled themselves into thinking that just because they have not ended a bad marriage by way of divorce, that somehow they are stellar examples of faith. I am not suggesting divorce is right in every case, however, I will say this: "it is as much a sin to be in a marriage that is a mockery of marriage than to end a marriage!" There is a better third option than to either kill the relationship or stay miserable. You could allow God to heal your relationship! If you want that in the form of a fortune cookie maybe we could say this, "marriage without intimacy is mockery!"

Straight Ahead friends. JT

41

Hope in Darkness

"The people who walk in darkness will see a great light, those who live in a dark land, The light will shine on them" (Isa. 9:2, referenced in Zacharias' prophesies of John the Baptist in Luke 1:79 referred to again by the Apostle Paul in 2 Corinthians 4:6).

I remember early on in ministry taking a group of teens and youth sponsors into a dark cave near New River in West Virginia. The week of camp was in partnership with Appalachian Bible College. We did what you always do in youth ministry. You have all the kids turn their flashlights off and you have them wave their hand in front of their face. You then have the group turn their flashlights on and everyone is relieved (except for those kids who were up to no good when it was dark.) You then give the ten-minute devotional using the light/dark motif to drive home a spiritual lesson. Typically, this is a favorite memory for the kids as they make it past the youth ministry and on into the college group. We learn from the book of Job that God's children can and do face deep seasons of darkness.

As the I pin this, I am doing a personal Bible study that is riveting. I am tracing the roots and occurrences of the Biblical terms for "darkness" and "light" in both the Old and New Testament. It may be some of you are hurting deeply and I mean deeply as you read this devotional. You need to understand that it's okay for you to be in a dark place because God wants you to face Him and learn to trust Him in the darkness, and He promises to lead you to Himself as you are drawn to the true Light.

Over the years, I have enjoyed taking a group of kids to our summer church camp in the White Mountains of Eastern Arizona. It's beautiful up there and gets us out of the heat of the Phoenix area. Often, we are at camp over the fourth of July week and, typically, I will go into Eager, AZ in the evening to enjoy the cool and the fireworks. There is a reason why most fireworks are shot off in the evening. The lights make a dazzling show against the backdrop of the darkness.

I'm confident God does the same thing in using the backdrop of dark hours in our lives to show off His light, grace and glory in your life and mine. He's teaching us some things we just would never learn in the same way if it was light and cheery all the time. You need to also understand that you must not become comfortable in the dark. Darkness, time and again in the Scriptures, alludes to Satan's playground. According to 2 Cor. 4:6 and a host of other Scriptures (like Isaiah 8:19-9:7), Christ came to smash Satan's darkness by the glorious love and light of Jesus - including shining His Light into your hurting heart tonight if you'll let him. It is in the darkness where shame thrives. It holds us captive until we bring it out into the light within loving relationships and find that the lies whispered into our ears by Satan are usually unfounded.

Often God's children, in the moment when darkness surrounds them, choose to take the easy route. Often out of bitterness and desperation, we just stuff the pain and cope with the darkness by traveling deeper into the darkness. Instead of facing our hearts towards God in submission to His plan (because often there is pain or fear there), we fight what He's doing. Instead of turning on the Light, we grab the quickest route to ease our pain. Our souls can become polluted and we will find ourselves stunned, stuck and alone. Like Job, we secretly long for "the end." Here's hope for you who are suffering in darkness - *"Light arises in the darkness for the upright; He is gracious and compassionate and righteous. It is well with the man who is gracious and lends; he will maintain his cause in judgment. For he will never be shaken; the righteous will be remembered forever. He will not fear evil tidings; his heart is steadfast trusting in the Lord. His heart is upheld, he will ot fear, until he looks with satisfaction on his adversaries. He has given freely to the poor; his righteousness endures forever; his horn will be exalted in honor. The wicked will see it and be vexed; he will gnash his teeth and melt away; the desire of the wicked will perish." (Ps. 112:4-10).* Remember this, the One who loves you and is light, is with you. You are not alone!

Straight Ahead friends! JT

42

Short-sighted Decision-Making

"And King Rehoboam consulted with the elders who had served his father Solomon while he was still alive, saying, 'How do you counsel me to answer this people? Then they spoke to him, saying, 'If you will be a servant to this people today, will serve them, grant them their petition, and speak good words to them, then they will be your servants forever.' But he forsook the counsel of the elders which they had given him, and consulted with the young men who grew up with him and served him." (I Ki. 12:6-8)

Rehoboam made a bad decision in ignoring the wise counsel of the older men who had served Solomon. It resulted in the Kingdom being split between the tribes of Israel and those of Judah. How do you move on in life after a bad decision?

In my book on *Decision-Making in Ministry*, I noted the occasion of Hitler sending in the German Army (The Wehrmacht) into Russia in June of 1941. Operation Barbarossa ended up in failure in large degree because Hitler ignored what should have been a clear lesson from Napoleon's failed attempt by his "Grande Armee" more than a century before. The Scriptures are full of examples for believers to note lessons from bad decision-making.

Consider Sarah (aka..."Sarai"). For the moment, she is not able to have children. In Genesis 16, we see her making a choice out of desperation, which she later regrets. She gives her husband Abram her servant Hagar with whom to have a child. Ishmael is the result of that union. Sarah, out of jealousy that Hagar might win some of Abram's affections and envy that Hagar can become pregnant, accuses Hagar of despising her now that Hagar is expecting and she is not. While this practice seems "odd" to the Western mindset today, this was a very common practice in the ancient near-east. There are pages and pages I could write on this episode, however, I want to pull out of this passage an important observation. Often, we make really bad decisions that impact us for years to come. Typically, we were desperate in the moment. We found ourselves in a tough situation and we grabbed the first thing that crossed our mind by way of opportunity without being careful or discerning.

When I wrote my book on decision-making a few years ago, I noted that "desperation is the mother of bad decision-making." I've seen believers and leaders leave churches for self-centered reasons. These dear believers who have made it a habit to complain about this and that at their church have done so in front of their children for years. The "kids" watched (and heard) as the family put its own activities in front of a first-level commitment to the community of believers. Almost always these kinds of believers flip and flop from "church-to-church" only to be shocked that when the kids get to their adult years, they watch as worship and corporate participation within a community of believers is the last thing on their children's minds. Sometimes the parents are amazed at what their own ambivalence and ecclesiastical consumerism to Christ's Body has sown in the lives of their offspring. Their children's attitudes reflect those they learned from mom and dad. I've watched young people pile on crazy debt for education or a wedding only to live under the weight of that bad decision for years to come. I've sat across the table from great people who decades after their wedding admitted, "I married the wrong person."

So, what happens when you make a bad decision and you're stuck with the implications of that decision?

(1) To start with, instead of beating yourself up, remember that there was a context for why you made that decision. Hindsight they say is 20-20. Frankly, often we think we made a bad decision but that is in part because we now know and see more of the picture than what we knew or saw at that time. In some cases, we really made the best decision we could with the facts as we knew them. In a sense, you were backed up to your Red Sea and you didn't have a staff that turned into a viper in the presence of the Egyptians. So you either had to turn and fight or make a bridge.

(2) Remember what man (including you) meant for evil, God can turn to good (Gen. 50:20, Rom. 8:28). Scripture is full of these kinds of events.

(3) The Genesis 50 passage demonstrates that, even though early on Joseph had made a wrong decision or two, because Joseph had a pure heart and followed God in faith (even though he was dumped in a hole, accused falsely of a crime, and sent unjustly to jail), he

eventually ends up second in command of the Egyptian empire (not bad).

(4) Trust that even though you made a short-sighted decision, God can forgive that and create beauty out of your struggle. In faith, make the best of today and trust that God's grace can make up for what the real prophet Joel calls the "years of locusts" (Joel 2:25).

Straight Ahead friends! JT

43

Leadership and Criticism

"Faithful are the wounds of a friend, but deceitful are the kisses of an enemy." (Prov. 27:6). Another striking passage on criticism is found in Ex. 15:24, *"And the people grumbled at Moses…"*

I don't know this, but I sometimes wonder if Moses wasn't secretly happy that it was given to Joshua to lead the children of Israel into the promised land. I've often thought, man if it were me, I'd be striking more than the rock if I had to lead a group like Moses had to lead. I would have been tempted to start with Aaron and work my way down using that massive rod of his! It is probably a given. The larger impact you have and the wider your influence grows, the more criticism you will face. Other leaders will even struggle when you strike out on your own or hesitate to do so when they think you should. British Prime Minister Margaret Thatcher (the "Iron Lady") in an attempt to encourage President Bush (the first) and his stand against Saddam

Hussein's invasion of Kawait, said to US President, "Remember George, this is no time to go wobbly."

A simple explanation for this is that most people are more opinionated than they are willing to take the lead. It just simply means that the more people follow you, the more varied will be the number of opinions about your leadership and, unfortunately, too often more of it will be negative than positive.

A clear example is the US presidential approval rating. Most presidents end up with about half the country approving (to some degree) the work of the leading national executive. I suppose the moral of the story is if you really need a high degree of approval in your area of work, you should probably stay away from politics.

One clear exception to the rule was John F. Kennedy, whose average approval rating was just about 70%. Of course, all it takes is one significant detractor to end your career and opinion polls fluctuate considerably. Other exceptions are seen in the approval score for Eisenhower that ranged between 77% and 47%. George H. Bush's approval rating ranged between 90% and 25%. Nixon's approval rating ranged between 66% and 24%. Scoring almost as low as the "Watergate President" is both Obama (between 60% and 38%), and Carter between (74% and 28%). At the time of this writing, President Trump's approval rating is at 47%. This is not surprising when one considers how divisive the last election cycle has been.

There is something of an unwritten rule in the universe teaching that criticism is an important discipline if you plan on being responsible in your leadership. Because most of us are hit at the emotional level when being criticized, you will often need help in evaluating the nature of that criticism and discerning if it is (1) a sound and reasonable complaint about a real weakness, (2) an unfair perception or (3) the result of selfish and petty envy by the one(s) being critical. Usually, you will not be able to satisfy your critic, who is simply envious.

You probably should learn to ignore the peanut gallery. Nay-sayers will always be jaundiced by those who act. When the famous German pastor Dietrich Bonhoffer told his family as a young man that he was going to study theology, his brothers mocked his choice. In a famous line the young Bonhoffer responded by saying, *"Dass es einen Gott gibt, daufer lass ich mir den Kopf abschlagen."* Which means, "even if you were to knock my head off, God would still exist" – (Bonhoffer, Metrax, p. 38).

You have an opportunity to save a healthy relationship with those who are reacting negatively to your weaknesses or even perceived weaknesses. You don't need to take their criticism personally. The reality is that if you are in leadership in any shape or form and have been there for some time, you probably are doing at least ten or fifteen things very well. Can't someone disagree with one area of your leadership without you jumping to the conclusion that they are rejecting all of your leadership or that they are turning their back on you completely? Even if at first you don't see the complaint as fair, learn to say "thank you" and try not to take their advice as a personal slam. You might even say something affirming like, "I will consider the possibility of my needing to pay closer attention to this." I have found that if you do this without sarcasm, the gossip and negative attitude often soon evaporates. If you can find even one thing this person is saying that is valid (you can agree with it) and you express this to them, this person will feel heard. Even if you cannot agree with even one tiny thing that has been said, you can validate their emotions, "I can see that this is really important to you, or, I can see that you feel really strongly about this." Again, this person will feel heard and their anger disarmed. This might also turn your "enemy" into an ally.

Remember often that there is an element of truth we can take away and from which we can benefit. If nothing else, you can tell the person "you'll consider" the observation in question. Strong leadership has the ability to hear that there might be room for growth.

Consider a few good quotes: "Criticism is something we can avoid easily by saying nothing, doing nothing and being nothing" (Aristotle). Perhaps my favorite quote on criticism comes from another President whose last name was Roosevelt. *"It is not the critic who counts; not the man who points out how the strong man stumbles, or where the doer of deeds could have done them better. The credit belongs to the man who is actually in the arena, whose face is marred by dust and sweat and blood, who strives valiantly; who errs and comes short again and again; because there is not effort without error and shortcomings; but who does actually strive to do the deed; who knows the great enthusiasm, the great devotion, who spends himself in a worthy cause, who at the best knows in the end the triumph of high achievement and who at the worst, if he fails, at least he fails while daring greatly. So that his place shall never be with those cold and timid souls who know neither victory nor defeat."* (Theodore Roosevelt)

Straight Ahead friends! JT

44

Know Yourself

"Let us examine and probe our ways, and let us return to the LORD." (Lam. 3:40).

Wikipedia has a great description of the famous Greek maxim, *"know thyself."* "...the proverb is applied to those whose boasts exceed what they are", and that "know thyself" is a warning to pay no attention to the opinion of the multitude."

So, here's a thought. "Know thyself", while certainly being connected to Ancient Greek thought, is not simply "Platonic." It is both Biblical and practical. The Psalmist notes, "...*I am fearfully and wonderfully made;*" (Ps 139:14). So, each of us have gifts, abilities and traits that are God-given. You can't do everything that sounds cool. To know ourselves fully is not possible because Jeremiah makes the point (Jer. 17:9) that *"The heart is more deceitful tan all else and is desperately sick; who can understand it?"* Sometimes we say after failing, "I meant well." You might think you meant well, but the human heart is such that you probably didn't entirely "mean well."

Biblically, there are at least two major ways we should consider ourselves. The first way is a view of self, which is submissive to our love for God and our pattern of having a righteous conscience. In other words, we need to work at training our affections. I have a friend who has written extensively about the issue of thinking about what you desire as a Christian and how those "tastes" can and should be submissive to our wills and, even more importantly, God's will. We need to consider as a believer if our tastes and the "things we like" are more consistent with our Lord or with our society. John reminds us to "stop loving the world" (1 Jn. 2:15). Frankly, that emphasis is a good one and is rarely talked about in evangelical circles.

The second way to consider ourselves is in connection with how I serve God at home, work, and service (church, society, etc...). Our conscience is trained in righteousness when we begin to take our thoughts captive as we submit our thinking to the subjection of Christ (2 Cor. 10:5). I have a dear friend who every ten years evaluates his calling, his gifts, and how his priority-passions have changed. He's now approaching seventy and he started doing this just before he was thirty. He told me recently that this practice has resulted in a change of ministry setting each time he has come to the ten-year mark. In other words, he has become sharper in his focus and that has resulted (at least for him) in a change of work setting. The result of this has been for him an increase in personal effectiveness because he uses more and more of his strengths and giftedness with each change of job setting.

While not suggesting we all pack up and move with the passing of each decade, I do think this sort of personal evaluation is good because we can easily fall into at least two "ruts." One extreme is when we do nothing until the perfect job or calling shows up. No, that's not right! Especially when you are younger, I think it's good to try a variety of things to find out exactly the kind of job or mission you are passionate about. At the other extreme is the guy or gal who is clueless about who they are. They seem to live life without a rudder. Because in our natural state our hearts are impacted by sin, we really can't fully "know ourselves" (Jer.17:9).

So maybe you find yourself now gun-shy because you thought you knew yourself (at least to some degree) but this last life-chapter was rough. Look, anyone can have a rough season. It doesn't mean you are clueless about yourself! If you are unsure, find a pastor, mentor or friend who loves you enough to be honest with you. They can help you with a healthy evaluation. Often, they will see strengths (and weaknesses) in you to which you are blinded. Ultimately, the best way to know yourself is to know God. Paul says this in Phil. 3:10, "*that I may know Him, and the power of His resurrection....*" He made us in His image and the closer we know and walk with God, the more clearly we can see our purpose and mission.

Ultimately, the best way to know yourself is to know God. Paul says this in Philippians 3:10, "*that I may know him and the power of his resurrection....*" He made us in His image and the closer we know and walk with God, the more clearly we can see our purpose and mission. There is simply no way to accomplish this except by prayer. Prayer doesn't change God's Will, it reveals it. Arthur Pink notes well that "*prayer is communion with God, so that there will be common thoughts between His mind and ours. What is needed is for Him to fill our hearts with His thoughts, and then His desires will become our desires flowing back to Him.*" Luther said concerning prayer, "*Prayer is not overcoming God's reluctance, but laying hold of His willingness.*"

Straight Ahead friends! JT

45

Progress for the Pilgrim

"For I delivered to you as of first importance what I also received, that Christ died, for our sins according to the Scriptures, and that He was buried, and that He was raised on the third day according to the Scriptures. And that He appeared to Cephas, then to the twelve. After that He appeared to more than five hundred brethren at one time, most of whom remain until now, but some have fallen asleep; then He appeared to James, then to all the apostles; and last of all, as it were to one untimely born, He appeared to me also." (1 Cor. 15:3-8).

It has been a continual struggle in ministry to remind people and even Christian leaders what is the heart and essence of Biblical Christianity. Biblical Christianity is about the sovereignty of God, the preeminence of Jesus, the centrality of the cross, the power of the Gospel, the faith of the believer, the promises and love of the Father, the forgiveness of the sinner, the potency of the Holy Spirit, the authority and sufficiency of the Scriptures, the protection of a redeemed Israel, the mission of a sent-out-church, the celebration of the resurrection, and the expected return of our victorious Savior. Our standing is not dependent on us! It is secured by the holiness of God, the sacrifice of Calvary, the plan of eternity, the imputed righteousness of the saints by the alien virtue of the Son of God, which blots out our personal failures as well as the guilt of Adam and secures our eternal standing by grace alone, through faith alone, in Christ alone, revealed by Scripture alone, for the glory of God alone! That my friend is good news (and maybe a bit of theology!)

An understanding of the Christian faith and how to live it is the heart cry of every Spirit-born Christian. It is our job to share our hope--the gospel--with those around us. You don't have to be good at it. You just need to be willing and able to share how Jesus rescued you from sin. Those around us need to understand the ABC's of the gospel. God is Holy. We are sinful. Jesus lived a moral life perfectly to be the ethical base of our forgiveness. Jesus 100 % God and 100% man, died on the cross for our sins. This atonement satisfied the Holy wrath of Heaven against our transgressions against God. Jesus of Nazareth defeated death and sin by literally and physically rising from the grace. One day He will return to rule and reign forever. We can have forgiveness only through faith in Christ and repentance of sin.

Powerful has been the effect on a simple allegory of the Christian life. In 1678, John Bunyan pinned from a simple desk in a Bedford jail *The Pilgrim's Progress*. This simple yet universal application of the faith to our walk has no doubt aided in it becoming the world's best-selling devotional book. Bunyan represents well the Puritan mindset of the Gospel life. I am thankful for the various groups, associations and denominations which still love God and have kept pure the

Gospel of Christ. I am thankful for a number of theological traditions that have done the same. However, none of those names and traditions deserve the honor or the loyalty that belong to Jesus, God's Word, and the Gospel alone. Whenever men (even good men) put their oar in the water, to some degree they will poison what is pure.

Thank God that the water of life comes freely from the hand of God to the heart of the believer. *"The rivers of life flow from the face and fingers of God. In His grace He brings us to know His heart through the love He brings into our life. When it's true the mark on the soul is unmistakable and eternal. To complete our growth into the image of His profitable children, He allows enough loss and pain to make us adore the beauty He eventually brings our way, the mercy of the gospel, the embrace of a friend, the whisper of the wind in the branches of the evergreen trees of life, the voice of a child laughing, the kiss of his presence. The most precious gifts are held deep in the sanctuary of our heart. These outstrip the worlds' finest gold. These go with us from this world to the last. Courage grows as we take the steps only heaven sees. It looks to the One in whose hands we dwell. He gives us the strength to hike on more day, one more mile and sometimes just one more moment…"* (Poem, *"The Rivers of Life"* by Joel Tetreau)

Straight Ahead friends! JT

46

The Benevolence of God

"I know how to get along with humble means, and I also know how to live in prosperity; in any and every circumstance I have learned the secret of being filled and going hungry, both of having abundance and suffering need." (Phil. 4:12).

This is Paul's way of saying (as he says elsewhere) that he is able to be right and to think right under times of blessing and during times of challenge.

Yesterday, I preached out of the book of Genesis. We are looking at the call of Abraham from Genesis 12, 13, and onward. Genesis is a full book. Later, in this opening book of the Torah, we read of Joseph. Joseph demonstrates well this principle to which Paul is speaking. Joseph demonstrated the ability to suffer (unjustly for years in a dusty jail), and he also demonstrated how to steward blessings (second in command of the Egyptian empire--talk about a swing of circumstances). I think we Bible teachers often spend time on how to rightly suffer but I don't think we spend enough time thinking about how we should handle the seasons of blessing. You will remember in Genesis 41 that we read the account of Joseph explaining to Pharaoh how to handle the responsibility associated with the years of plenty (seven fat cows!) He advised Pharaoh to store away the extra during the years of plenty to help with the years of famine (seven gaunt cows.) If you are experiencing blessing, you will remember that God told Abraham one of the reasons for God's covenant with Abraham was not only for Abraham and his descendants to be "blessed" but to "bless!" (*"...and in you all the families of the earth shall be blessed."* - Gen 12:3b)

Robert Gilmour LeTourneau died June 1, 1969. The world knew LeTourneau as the famous businessman whose name was on much of the world's heavy moving equipment. However, Robert had a far more passionate drive and that was God's work here on earth. He set aside 90% of his salary to fund ministry and he lived off 10%. LeTourneau faithfully served in his church and denomination (Christian & Missionary Alliance). His personal biography explains that the more he gave away to God's work, the more God blessed his company.

So, we might ask the question, "How should I respond in the season of blessing?" I think, for starters, there are two answers to that question.

First, we must remain thankful for the blessings of life. Understand you have friends and loved ones who live with challenges every day that we take for granted. God does not owe us anything! Our health is an unbelievable gift. Most of us in the Western world are wealthy beyond imagination compared to the rest of the globe and especially compared to those who lived centuries before us.

Second, I am reminded of our responsibility laid out in Galatians 6:10 when the Apostle Paul reminds us "*...let us do* *good to all men, and especially to those who are of the household of faith.*" Just a few verses earlier, we are reminded to "lift-up one another's burdens", for this is how we fulfill the Law of Christ (love God and love neighbor.)

Are you blessed and unaware of it? Some of you reading this would admit life is good and yet you continue to live life in rebellion against the God of Heaven. You my friend are living on borrowed time. There is a verse in the Bible that may have been written just for you: "*Or do you think lightly of the riches of His kindness and forbearance and patience, not knowing that the kindness of God leads you to repentance?*" (Rom. 2:4). The rest of the passage explains that when God has been good to you and you refuse to repent of sin and follow Christ in faith, all you are doing is hardening your heart and storing up the wrath of God for the Day of Judgment. You should repent. Really. Those of us who have and are experiencing blessings should be thankful.

Straight Ahead friends! JT

47

This World is Not my Home

"...O LORD, the God of our fathers, are You not God in heaven, and do You not rule over all the kingdoms of the nations, art Thou not God in the heavens? And art Thou not ruler over all the kingdoms of the nations? Power and might are in Thy hand so that no one can stand against Thee. Didst Thou not, O our God, drive out the inhabitants of this land before Thy people Israel, and give it to the descendants of Abraham Thy friend forever?" (2 Chron. 20:6-7).

The context of this passage is a powerful one. The offspring of Lot, namely Moab and Ammon, along with the descendants of Esau, had their eyes on the throne of Judah. God sent a message to Judah by way of His prophet Jahaziel. The message was, "I will destroy your enemies." It happened just as God said it would. The king of Judah, Jehoshaphat, was a God-minded leader. It's clear in this passage that he understood that the Lord is "King of the Universe."

Perhaps the most famous music written by George Friedrich Handel was the *Messiah*, written in 1741 and performed for the first time during Lent on April 13, 1742 in Dublin, Ireland. Tradition tells us that when the "Hallelujah Chorus" was presented in London for the first time, King George II stood to his feet. Of course, the apex of the "Hallelujah Chorus" is the praise of the Messiah who is "King of Kings and Lord of Lords." To this day it is a regular practice for audiences to stand during the "Hallelujah Chorus."

Daniel 2:21 reminds us that "He [*God*] *removes kings and establishes kings*," Daniel 4:17, "…That *the Most High is ruler over the realm of mankind, and bestows it on whom He wishes, and sets over it the lowliest of men.*" Apparently, Daniel thinks that even when the executive and judicial branches of government are anti-God, God is still very much in control of those governments. When laws are anti-God, they have a shelf-life that will only last if God uses their twisted presence. Eventually, unless those governments & the nations they represent repent, He "wads" those governments up like yesterday's trash, throws them away, and creates a new government to take their place.

Often the health and life-span of governments are, directly or indirectly, tied to how they treat God's people, either the Church or Israel. So, here's an implication. Some of us have believed that a democracy/republic is a Biblical approach to government and as such it is taught in (or at least demonstrated by) the Scriptures. In one sense, I see a democracy/republic more consistent with God's character than other forms of government, but I think we can see a democracy or republic is only as Biblical, and effective, as the culture or the godliness of the people who govern the nation. The same thing can be said of a free-market approach to economics. To the degree that Biblical principles govern that approach to commerce, it is to that same degree it will reflect godly characteristics. The reality is God's people, regardless if we are talking about Israel in the old covenant or the Church in the new covenant, can thrive during any government and any economic system. Ultimately, one day we will all be blessed because we will get to live in a theocracy with Jesus on the throne.

You need a modern-day example? Okay, how about a hundred million (or more) Christians doing "body-life" in China today right under the nose of an atheistic communist government? You want an ancient example? Okay, how about Daniel being promoted to the highest level of three consecutive super powers amid the Jewish exile? Having pagan heads of state giving public and official declarations about the "god" of Daniel being "the God" of the universe (proclamations that even make it into the Hebrew text of the Old Testament no less!) That's impressive. I'm guessing Babylon had some twisted courts! You want another ancient example? How about a Persian King (Cyrus) giving a decree in 538 B.C. for the rebuilding of Jerusalem and the Temple (begun in 536 B.C. and completed in 516 B.C). This is the same Cyrus whose son was Darius; whose grandson was Xerxes (he's called King Ahasuerus in the book of Esther), and whose great-grandson was Artaxerxes. These guys weren't Baptist! Having said that, it's clear God used this line of pagan kings to rescue God's people on more than one occasion.

So, it's been a blessing to have a government that in principle has been pro-Christian in many ways. If that season is over (and it may be over), now we will have to minister in the context of a government that is frankly hostile to Christianity and very secular. That just means that the church in America will have to endure pretty much what all believers have had to always endure—living a Christian life in a place that is not our home. While a few things have changed, ultimately nothing has changed. God was faithful then, He'll be faithful now.

Straight Ahead friends! JT

48

Being Quiet with God

"But the LORD is in His holy temple. Let all the earth be silent before Him" (Hab. 2:20). *"...in repentance and rest you shall be saved, in quietness and trust is your strength."* (Isa. 30:15). *"Cease striving and know that I am God."* (Ps. 46:10).

The Gospels record the practice of Jesus going off by Himself, away from people and spending time alone in prayer with God. One of those episodes is recorded in Luke 6:12 – 13. During Jesus' ministry in Galilee, our Lord went up on a mountain alone to pray. When He came off the mountain the next day, He chose His disciples.

We also need solitude and silence as individuals. God made us that way. Don Whitney notes that *"one of the costs of technological advancement is a greater temptation to avoid quietness"* (*Spiritual Disciplines*, p. 228).

Over the years, I have enjoyed hunting. One of the real benefits of being in a deer blind for hour after hour is the ability you have to quiet your mind. I always would take a pen and paper pad with me because inevitably, as I would be quiet, the Lord would impress on my mind a variety of things. The things I had been reading and studying would often blossom in front of me with a variety of implications I simply could not see when amid the typical daily "noise." One of the best gifts husbands of wives who have small children can give their wife is an hour or two or three of quiet. When the kids were little, I would take them to McDonalds to eat and play in the balls. We would then go to the nearby grocery store that had free childcare. The kids would play in the "kid's corner" while I would study and enjoy a second cup of coffee and something to eat from the deli. After we were done, I would purchase a gallon of milk and take it home because we were out of milk at the house. Toni would have had several hours of respite. The relief in her eyes was priceless to me.

Our bodies, minds, and spirits simply need quiet. It's why at our church, we have decided not to have Sunday evening service. We pack the morning on Sunday with ministry and meetings and practice and worship so that, after our lunch, we can enjoy the rest of the day for a real "day of rest." Over the years, some have called this a "Sabbath's rest." I personally believe this kind of thing honors the spirit behind the Mosaic Law concept for Sabbath. It was for both corporate rest and spiritual quiet. In too many ministries, the leadership core never allows itself to be quiet. They are always doing ministry and the threat with that is, if we don't allow our minds and spirits a time of refreshment, it's possible to fall into the trap of ministry as routine instead of worshipping in "Spirit and in Truth." That's not a shot at assemblies that choose to have a Sunday evening service. We find that the free afternoon and evening is good for our families for real times of rest and reflection. Often, families will also use that time for fellowship.

On the other extreme are found those who have taken quiet as an excuse to just isolate away from people or cease to be involved with others altogether. When you swing the pendulum either way, you end up hurting yourself.

Modern technology has helped us in so very many ways. One way it can hurt us is if we are not careful, we can be "plugged-in" too much. The problem with always keeping your smart phone or your lap top right by your head every waking (or sleeping) moment, is that your body and spirit don't get the alone time it desperately needs. When you don't get your "un-plugged" time in, you are depleted as an individual meaning that you don't have all that you need to have to give to others. I've had to learn this as a pastor and as a leader who helps other leaders. If I'm not scheduling any away time to be alone with God and myself, I will burn myself out in life and ministry and I'll be no help to those who I must and want to help. In order to give all that you can to others, you need significant time (both real time and cyber time) away from others. Jesus demonstrates this over and over in His ministry. Are you "stressed out" because you are too "plugged in?" Here's an idea--turn those gadgets off for a day or two and see what that does for you.

Straight Ahead friends! JT

49

Discerning Advice

Proverbs 1:5, *"A wise man will hear and increase learning, and a man of understanding will acquire wise counsel...."* Proverbs 9:8, *"Do not reprove a scoffer, lest he hate you, reprove a wise man, and he will love you."* Proverbs 29:9, *"When a wise man has a controversy with a foolish man, the foolish man either rages or laughs, there is no rest."*

In 1793, William Carey set sail from England to India along with fellow missionary John Thomas. The two men were headed off to take the message of the Gospel to a spiritually dark portion of Asia. Interesting to note that just a few years earlier in his gospel preparation while presenting his heart for gospel outreach William was told, "Young man, sit down; when God is pleased to convert the heathen world, He will do it without your help or mine." Thank God, Carey ignored that bit of bizarre and twisted advice! Most of us get unwanted, unsolicited "advice" from family, friends, and "others" from time to time. So, what do you do with that?

I've noted three passages that give us some clarity. These passages (and many others found in the Scriptures) give us some starting points with "unwanted advice."

First, even if you are not sure of the motive behind the one giving the advice, wisdom will allow you to fairly consider the observation presented even if the giving of it is, in small part or even large part, given unfairly. Let's remember this, if one person has a perspective on a part of our character that is less than flattering, it's a good bet they aren't the only one that shares that view. Certainly, we can learn and change something?

Second, there is something right about the giving and receiving of advice when the motives on both sides are healthy.

Third, if it is clearly foolish advice you are getting from foolish people, usually you are best to ignore the noise and move on.

Not long before Carey left London for India, the British Empire would be rocked by the tenacious conviction of an evangelical Anglican lawmaker by the name of William Wilberforce. Even though he was the target of ridicule from every corner of the empire, Wilberforce pressed forward with his conviction concerning the evil of slavery. Finally, in 1833, a month after his death, the British House of Commons voted to abolish the British institution of slavery. Early on, William had been given countless words of advice on the importance of dropping his legal quest. He was told time and again that his foolish quest, while noble, was simply not practical. Not too long into his work, he had listened to the heart-felt encouragement of pastor and hymn-writer John Newton who had been saved out of a life of slave-trading and who was the writer of the beautiful hymn, "Amazing

Grace." It was of God that Wilberforce ignored the wrong advice and listened to wise advice.

A final thought. Sometimes people's advice is good but the timing of the implementation of that advice is bad. Even in a case like that, you most always can look the person in the eye and thank them for caring enough that they were willing to share. If you don't plan to take them up on their thoughts, it's not necessary to tell them that unless they make it a habit of being a pest and in your business "all the time." In that case you might let them know that if you ever need their thoughts on a matter, you'll call them "straight away."

Another thought, while it might not be the right time to implement their suggestion, if that suggestion is a worthwhile and good suggestion, you might want to thank them and explain that this is a great idea but implementing it will need to wait.

Straight Ahead friends! JT

50

Know-it-all Neighbor

Numbers 12:1 notes.... "Then *Miriam and Aaron spoke against Moses because of the Cushite woman whom he had married*...(notice verse 10)...*behold Miriam was leprous,...*". God says in Psalm 101:5, "*Whoever secretly slanders his neighbor, him I will destroy*;"

Some will say a good rule of thumb is to never say something about someone else unless you are first willing to say it to their face. Another way of saying that is treat your neighbor with kindness. I think a better thing to do is, if you're going to say something hard about a neighbor, say it to them directly and do it with a commitment to speaking truth in love.

Let me give an area where this is especially important. It is important that we honor the sacred nature of "other" families. This is why it is important to use wisdom in how we speak concerning other pastors and other ministries. When you see a family (or another ministry) doing something that you would not do...how do you handle that? Do you leave that to them and God and trust there is more that you probably don't know to that episode or do you become "judge and jury" and mete out emotional justice (like Miriam did) as you slander and gossip about "such-and-such" family? You will notice in the opening passage, Miriam just knew she had the right view of Moses' new wife. It is interesting that in Titus 2:3, Paul warns older women in the church to resist the temptation to slander. It's also interesting that Paul tells women in leadership or women whose spouses are in leadership to avoid the sin of slander (1 Tim. 3:11). Perhaps if men often struggle with the temptation of lust, some women will struggle with the temptation to slander.

James 5 tells us that we all will struggle with our tongue (speech) to one degree or another. Your tongue can be lethal! It contains poison and has a flammable capacity to burn and destroy. The point is this, when something happens in a different family, it's probably best to assume there is more happening then what you and I know. That family, not your family, is in many cases in the best place to determine what to do or not to do. They are aware of sensitivities that none of us know and it's consistent to respect the sanctity of that family by assuming the best and by praying and hoping the best for them instead of setting in judgment as some familial quarterback whose personal family is quote-in-quote "perfect."

I've watched several families who just knew that their schooling approach for children coupled with home-made bread, mandatory livestock chores, and a host of other "practices" would produce a consistent set of offspring that would honor God. Sadly, in several cases the adult offspring's life demonstrated just the opposite. This kind of law over grace approach to parenting resulted in children running and escaping into the "world". In other cases, some children have simply become more "Amish" and frankly less "Christian." Please note that training children in a behavioristic way, while effective in the world of Ivan Pavlov, isn't the way to produce children for Christ. If we are close and we are concerned, there is nothing wrong with letting them know we are here to help if they need it. However, don't be a "know-it all" and just bust into the privacy of their family-life assuming you know best. The truth is you probably don't know best. As Walter Cronkite used to say, "and that's the way it is!"

Straight Ahead friends! JT

51

Hitting Re-set

"The Lord is my shepherd I shall not want." (Ps. 23:1)

Several years ago, I had the privilege of preaching several messages on Psalm 23. I think it took me 5 months. What a rich passage. We noted a list of implications--one of which was the issue of fear. Because the Lord is my shepherd, He's with me, He protects me and my life and everything about it is in His hands.

That's why in Dt. 31:6, Moses reflects on his strength and courage because of God's presence. Moses gave this same message to Joshua (Jos. 1:3-9). David passed this same message onto Solomon (1 Chr. 28:20). Isaiah was also given this same message (Isa. 41:13). Jesus told His disciples to not fear those who hated them (Mt. 10:28). The Apostle Paul reminds us that the spirit of fear is not from heaven and it's not necessary because "Abba" will protect you. Paul told Timothy the same thing (2 Tim. 1:7). The Philippians were reminded that struggle and persecution, if it does anything, makes us even bolder (Phil. 1:14-21)! Barnabas (or whoever you think wrote Hebrews) makes it clear that because God never abandons His children and He by nature is the helper of His children, we simply do not need to fear (Heb. 13:5-6)! Peter tells us the same thing (1 Pet. 3:13-14). John reminds us that love and fear aren't compatible (1 John 4:18).

All of us struggle to one degree or another with this. Thankfully, God's grace is sufficient my friends. Remember that understanding the power and faithfulness of our God coupled with a clarity on our "mission" will ultimately result in courage. "*Remember therefore from where you have fallen, and repent and do the deeds you did at first;...* " (Rev. 2:5a). This helps us in "real time" because all of us have disappointments that we must face. There is no "free pass" out of those challenges.

Think of the moon. Do you know why the moon is scarred with all those "potholes"? Yeah, because it's moving too slow to be able to avoid those God-made asteroids and comets that smack into its surface on a regular basis. So just like the moon, our inward man picks up these marks from hurts and other challenges that come our way.

Surviving the barrage of disappointments in life is in part the result of learning how to think about those when they come your way. This is especially true when you have a season during which it feels like the attacks are coming from all sides. It's like we are on the receiving end of an intense blitzkrieg.

Let me give you a suggestion on at least a partial response based upon John's inspired thoughts for the church in Ephesus. After commending the congregation for a variety of strengths, God challenges this group concerning losing its first-love and priority for the Lord. In responding to that, Jesus encourages the group to "...do the deeds you did at first..." When you and I face challenges that catch us by surprise, we must remember that usually we cannot in a minute, or an hour, a day, or even in a week, (and sometimes never) completely turn the situation around so that it disappears altogether. However, usually there are one or two things that we can do right away. Often, these are things we have done before to help us succeed in the area of challenge. Here's what you will find. Start out with the one or two things you can do today and watch how quickly those items will result in the accomplishment of the rest of "the fix." Often times, by doing the one or two things that are in your power (by God's strength)...God will pick it up from there and bring the rest of the crises to a close. Have a great week, my friends.

Straight Ahead! JT

52

Working Hard - Hardly Working

"It is good for a man to bear that he should bear the yoke in his youth." (Lam. 3:27)

My father believed that! His father believed that. My great-grandfather believed that. For decades, the Michigan wing of the Tetreau family made their living by building houses out of field stones. Much of the rest of the family farmed. All of that was hard work.

As a Christian leader, it concerns me that we are too often failing our young people in passing on the work ethic they will need in life. Yes, God will provide work and the means to provide for our families, but humanly speaking, it means we must get off our rear-ends, roll up our sleeves, and learn how to work hard to the glory of God. If our children have an "entitlement mentality", they will learn the hard way that nothing comes to them without being responsible in the area of employment. You have to want it, find it, work it, to keep it! Ecclesiastes 9:10 and other passages remind us that whatever our hands find to do, we need to give it our best efforts.

The Scriptures give us a variety of other principles concerning work. Work is ordained of God (Gen. 1). Work is for a lifetime (Gen. 3:19). Work is not punishment, but God's plan for all of us (Eccl. 2:24-25). Work is honorable (1 Cor. 10:31). The Bible gives us a variety of other principles concerning God's view of our labor.

I want to leave you with one more principle. especially for young people looking to head into the work place for the first time. Proverbs 25:6-7 is an interesting passage where Solomon explains that when in the presence of the king or someone who has rightly earned this standing, instead of exalting yourself prematurely, let the king exalt you in his time. This is much better than having to be demoted because you promoted yourself too soon. If you apply this principle to the context of employment, I think an implication is that it might be better for you to find a good company with maybe a lower level job than to find a great job with a lower level company. In other words, unless God leads you to start something new and He leads you instead to work under someone else's leadership, you are better off finding a boss (a king) who is successful and wise. Work humbly under his leadership and allow him to see your value resulting in God's timing for promotion in this healthy environment.

I remember asking my dad once why he chose to work in some of the places he did. I'll never forget his response. He told me that early on he had heard someone else say that they wanted to work with one of "God's good men." That's consistent with what we see here. Sometimes this isn't applicable because God opens just one door and the Lord makes it clear that you need to take a step of faith into a situation that you might think for the moment is less than ideal. However, when trying to determine God's best, consider that sometimes what might look best in the short-term may not be best in the long-term. If you are as sharp as you think you are, you will make promotion because good companies value good workers. If you start off and the company isn't quality, you'll be looking for a new job anyway. Just a Biblical thought with a practical application.

Straight Ahead! JT

53

Strength in Weakness

"Thus says the LORD, 'Let not a wise man boast of his wisdom, and let not the mighty man boast of his might, let not a rich man boast of his riches; but let him who boasts boast of this, that he understands and knows Me, that I am the LORD who exercises loving-kindness, justice, and righteousness on earth; for I delight in these things,' declares the LORD." (Jer. 9:23-24)

Too many of us depend on what I call the "cage-fighting" approach to life, home, and mission (which is what I refer to as the specific God-given tasks He has equipped you to do for the sake of God's kingdom). The problem with being "the dude" that kicks everyone's tail today by way of your own muscle is that you will eventually meet someone who has more muscle than do you! The prophet Nahum, 150 years after the events captured by the book of Jonah, spoke against Assyria explaining that their God-defying days were almost over. After about 300 years of Assyrian domination, the brutal empire fell in 607 B.C, giving way to the Babylonians.

There is a riveting passage in Zeph. 2:13-14, *"And He will stretch out His hand against the north and destroy Assyria, and He will make Nineveh a desolation, parched like the wilderness. And flocks will lie down in her midst, all beasts which range in herds; both the pelican and the hedgehog will lodge in the tops of her pillars; birds will sing in the window, desolation will be on the threshold; for He has laid bare the cedar work."* Well, that happened. Today, if you go to the east bank of the Tigris River, all that's left of the glory of Assyria are massive mounds of ruins where once stood the proud capital and an equally arrogant people. History is clear: if you depend on just your own strength and ignore a real dependence on the God of Heaven, your future isn't very bright. Those of us who at the end of the day primarily depend on our own talent, people-skills, intelligence, or even resources will eventually come to the end of our rope, in large part because we simply don't have enough rope! Without a doubt, it is God who has given us those gifts and abilities. Certainly, with those we are to bear our own load (Gal. 6:5) as well as the burdens of others (Gal. 6:2).

Let's remember that we must look to Jesus for strength because there simply will be days when we just don't have any. In those seasons of life, it's good to remember that Jesus tells us to *"Come unto Me, all who are weary and heavy-laden, and will give you rest."* (Mt. 11:28). I love Prov. 3:5-6..."*Trust in the Lord with all your heart, and do not lean on your own understanding. In all your ways acknowledge Him, and He will make your path straight."* I am so thankful that *"He has not dealt with us according to our sins, nor rewarded us according to our iniquities. For as high as the heavens are above the earth, so great is His lovingkindness toward those who fear Him."* (Ps. 103:10-11).

All of us, myself included, have had those occasions when our prayers have turned into more complaining or even accusing than beseeching. I can remember on more than one occasion reminding the Lord that the thing that just happened or the thing that just did not happen, was in fact (in case He was not paying attention) "not fair!" The next time we are tempted to accuse the Lord of not giving us what is fair--the more Biblical side of our mind should remind the more emotional side of our mind—just how grateful we should be that God does not give us what is fair or what we deserve!

Straight Ahead friends! JT

54

Parent-Child Relationship

"There is a kind of man who curses their father, and does not bless their mother" (Prov. 30:11).

Over the last couple of years in my counseling ministry, I've dealt with at least 5 different situations that centered on the "parent – child" relationship before, during, or after the adult son or daughter moved out on their own. What I've discovered is an unusual amount of confusion on a few facts that are straight forward in the text of Scripture. Here are a few reminders for all of us who are on different ends of these spectrum. (By the way, I don't mention this to single out anyone I'm dealing with or have dealt with). These are good reminders for any of us with young adult children who believe in Biblical values.

1) Your parents are always your parents and according to passages in both testaments (Ex. 20:12 & Eph. 6:2), they are always to be honored, even (and maybe especially) when you don't think they deserve that.

2) When a child is no longer "dependent," that is, for his lodging, food, vehicle, health insurance, education, etc., when he/she is out, all on "his/her own," then and only then is a child rightly (and I would even say Biblically) able to do that which they want to do--no matter their mom and dad's opinion. If you need help with that, consider this, what about young people who have been given the gift of celibacy? Must they be under the authority of their parents their whole lives, as some preach? No, that's bad theology and it's not consistent with Scripture. Technically, if you are still dependent on Mom and Dad, still living under their roof, to some degree you are still under the obligation to be compliant with mom and dad's rules or desires until you move out. Once the child is totally on their own, parents not only need to allow their adult children to make their own decisions but must not step in and rescue them from the consequences of foolish decisions when they have ignored or refused wise counsel.

Having said that, a wise parent is the one who allows a gradual ramping-up of independence on the part of the developing young person so that, by the time they are college age, they are clearly almost, if not largely, able to be self-determinant.

3) When a young person marries, that person's primary loyalty is to his or her spouse, not their parents (Gen 2:24 and Mt. 19:5). Practically this means that it is wrong, mom and dad, if you try to boss your married young person around. On the other hand, young people, it's wrong to throw your independence around in the face of mom and dad. There needs to be respect and a working at this from both sides. I'm not sure what happens more often, but I have witnessed parents that have an unhealthy sense of demand on

married children. There also are young married people who have a sense that they can demand, expect, and are entitled to receive help, usually financial, from their parents. That's just odd.

If you are old enough to make the decision to marry and have children, you are old enough to pay your own bills. If that means you both get a job, you do that. If that means you both get two jobs, you can do that too. It's not wrong for mom and dad to help, but it's wrong for you to demand that mom and dad must help. One last thought. Nothing is more disgusting than Christian people fighting over and making a fuss over their parents' estate for personal gain after Mom and Dad have passed on into Heaven. I understand fighting to protect what Mom and Dad desired, but that is different than being selfish and nasty demanding you get as much of the loot as you can grab for yourself and your kids. I have told my parents nothing would make me happier than for them to spend up whatever my potential side of the inheritance is on cruises and enjoying life! A few important thoughts.

Straight Ahead friends! JT

55

Handling Criticism

"And when His own people heard of this, they went out to take custody of Him; for they were saying, 'He has lost His senses.' And the scribes who came down from Jerusalem were saying, 'He is possessed by Beelzebul," and 'He casts out the demons by the ruler of the demons.'" (Mk. 3:21-22)

How do you handle criticism? In this passage, Jesus gets criticism from two groups: family members and faith leaders. So often, we deserve a part of the criticism we are getting. Another way of saying that is a wise man gains value from critics even when the critics do not have his best interest at heart. However, here ,Jesus deals with unfair criticism. There were times in Jesus' ministry He did not respond to fools. On this occasion here, He responded. The family members were wanting to restrain ("*kroteo*"--literally "arrest") Jesus because they thought He was crazy. The faith leaders were accusing Him of being controlled by Satan.

In response to the faith leaders, Jesus simply reminds them that it makes no sense that He would be controlled by

Satan because He is destroying Satan's house. We read His words in verse 25, *"And if a kingdom is divided against itself, that kingdom cannot stand."* Jesus then goes on to explain to the twisted faith leaders that they were guilty of the ultimate blasphemy, the unpardonable sin. To His family members who obviously forgot the whole Temple experience when Jesus was 12, reminded them that His spiritual blood connections with believers was closer, if not even more important, than biological family blood connections.

A few final thoughts about criticism - The Harrison Postulate is "for every action, there is an equal and opposite criticism!" Elbert Hubbard noted, "to avoid criticism, do nothing, say nothing, be nothing." Ralph W. Emerson is quoted to have said, "Whatever you do, you need courage. Whatever course you decide upon, there is always someone to tell you are wrong. There are always difficulties arising which tempt you to believe that your critics are right. To map out a course of action and follow it to an end requires some of the same courage which a soldier needs. Peace has its victories, but it takes brave people to win them." Usually, people who are characterized by a spirit of criticism aren't the brightest bulbs in the box! The very fact they are taken over with a critical spirit means they will be lacking the time or effort to constructively build on their own. Typically, that means very little that they do has lasting impact. It's much easier to tear down something someone else has done than to build that which is new.

Joseph Parker stepped into the pulpit of the City Temple in London for his Thursday sermon and announced that he was under some trepidation that day because of a letter he had received. It seemed that a gentleman wrote to tell Parker that he would be in the congregation that day for the express purpose of making a philosophical analysis of the sermon. After a long pause, Parker said, "I may add that my trepidation is somewhat mitigated by the fact that the gentleman spells philosophical with an 'f.' (Wycliffe Handbook of Preaching & Preachers, Moody, 1984, p. 214.) This simply reminds us that sometimes it doesn't matter that you have critics.

Straight Ahead friends! JT

56

Your Corner of His Vineyard

"And when they received it, they grumbled at the landowner, saying, 'These last men have worked only one hour, and you have made them equal to us who have borne the burden and the scorching heat of the day. But he answered and said to one of them, 'Friend, I am doing you no wrong; did you not agree with me for a denarious? Take what is yours and go your way, but I wish to give to this last man the same as to you." (Mt. 20:11-14)

In Mathew 20:1-16, we read the Parable of the Landowner/Vineyard Owner. Because of the effects of our fallen natures, we all struggle with pride to one degree or another. Some of us are sinfully proud of our accomplishments or abilities. There are many who strut around knowing that they are most certainly some of God's "pretty people." Some of us struggle with what I call "intellectual arrogance." Many in this latter category are under the delusional effect that because they are academically more talented (or degreed) than others, they must add more to God's kingdom.

Here in this passage, Jesus knows that many Jews struggled with self-righteousness. We often think this was characteristic of the Pharisees (and it was) but we forget even the Apostles had internal arguments as to who would be most important in and for the sake of the Kingdom (notice Mt. 18:1-5). This continues to be a struggle in certain cultures. Many Asian cultures have assumed that if you have earned more credentials, that this somehow makes your position automatically more important. Often, it simply makes you more arrogant and less helpful. Too many have a head full of data and a heart full of pride.

Not too much has changed in the last 2000 years. Too many pastors, missionaries, and church members measure their worth by comparing ourselves with ourselves. This practice is clearly stupid according to Scripture (2 Cor. 10:12). It's not just Christian leaders who compare themselves to others. Women do this all the time--even Christian women. I will be speaking to this tendency by my sisters in Christ in the upcoming Mother's Day sermon later this year. Men do this as well. Teenagers do this. We think that our legacy and effect is dependent only on our work, our time in grade, or our greater and wider leadership and stewardship over larger and larger sections of the Lord's Vineyard. We think our success is defined by how many people know of us or like us. How many "friends" we have on social media. Well, Jesus dashes that idea to pieces in Mt. 20:11-14. No, it doesn't matter if the Lord hired you at 9 am, noon, 3 pm or even 5 pm. He, not you, determines when you serve, to whom you serve, how long you serve, how many people even know you serve, where you serve, and how much you will be compensated because you serve. In other words, it's all by grace!

Jesus knew that many believing Jews would struggle as the age of the Apostles would merge into the Church Age and the offer of salvation by grace would be given not just to Jews but also to Gentiles.

So the next time you look at your work in the Lord's vineyard and you are tempted to think that your family, popularity, effort or time in grade is insufficient, remember ultimately those details are not up to you. Jesus is the lover of our souls and Jesus is the Lord of the Harvest. He does all things well and we can trust Him! The question is this, will we be content to faithfully live out the mission He has given us in His Vineyard.

Straight Ahead my friends! JT

57

The Bread of Life

"Jesus therefore said to them, 'Truly, truly, I say to you, it is not Moses who has given you the bread out of heaven, but it is My Father who gives you the true bread out of heaven. For the bread of God is that which comes down out of heaven, and gives life to the world.' They said therefore to Him, 'LORD, evermore give us this bread.' Jesus said to then, 'I am the bread of life; he who comes to Me shall not hunger, and he who believes in Me shall never thirst." (Jn. 6:32-35)

Jesus is the Bread of Life! Why Bread?

The Hebrew word for "bread" (lehem) is used 297 times in the Old Testament. The Greek term for "bread" (artos) is used 99 times in the New Testament. In the ancient near east, bread was an important staple of everyday life. So much of society revolved around the making, preparation, and consuming of "bread." A Jewish meal often would begin with the father of the family taking a loaf, thanking God for His provision, and then breaking and sharing it with his family. Often "bread" was a reference to what we understand as "bread." Other times the use of the word "bread", while speaking of a meal, also pointed to a larger reference than simply a meal, such as an expression of hospitality. Many of us will say, "let's break bread together." While the reference includes a meal, the saying goes beyond simply consuming calories and touches upon the rich experience of fellowship. If this kind of thing is important to us, it was even more important in the ancient near east. One cannot read the Gospels without realizing how much of the Lord's ministry was accomplished while sharing a meal.

Another use of the word "bread" was an expression of God's bounty and blessing. An example of this is seen in Lk. 15:17, "...have more than enough bread..." Other uses of bread were as part of the corporate worship for the covenant community events, such as Passover and its use of unleavened bread and Pentecost with its use of two loafs of leavened bread. According to Exodus 12:39, Israel ate unleavened bread because the nation was hurried out of Egypt. From then onward, Jews would eat this, "bread of affliction" (Dt. 16:3) at the Feast of Unleavened Bread to remember the significance historically and spiritually of Passover. Also seen in the Old Testament was the Levite's use of showbread in the tabernacle (Ex. 25:23-30). Combined with this was the blessing of Manna for Israel in the Negev wilderness, where it was viewed as bread from heaven in abundance (Ps. 105:40; Neh. 9:15). With all these uses of the term bread, it's no wonder that Christ would use it as a powerful metaphor to speak of Himself.

In his teaching in Capernaum after the feeding of the five-thousand, Jesus proclaimed Himself to be the Bread of God that came from heaven (John 6:32-33, which was a reference of Ex. 16:4; and Ps. 78:24). Later in His earthly ministry, Jesus broke bread to represent that His body would soon be broken. We memorialize this as we partake of communion and the Lord's table. For this reason, the taking of bread (with juice or wine) is the most intimate expression of love and worship with our Lord. The many believers who form the body of Christ are blessed to partake in this bread. Indeed, Jesus is the Bread of Life!

Straight Ahead friends. JT

58

True Friendship

"A friend loves at all times, and a brother is born for adversity." (Prov. 17:17) *"A man of many friends comes to ruin, but there is a friend who sticks closer than a brother."* (Prov. 18:24)

Recently, I had the privilege of communicating God's forgiveness and my forgiveness of a brother who had failed ethically. He was very broken over his failure. I hugged his neck and we both cried over the failure, but we both rejoiced together over the marvelous cleansing mercy of our Father and, in his case, restoration with other believers. It was easy. You see I'm at the top of the list for sinners who have been forgiven, so when others admit failure, it's a piece of cake to forgive them. It's also because a friendship that is a true friendship is characterized by many things, chief among them is a willingness, or even an eagerness to forgive.

There is hardly a better picture of the Father's willingness and expectation of what true forgiveness looks like than the Gospel-picture of the father running to his repentant prodigal son in Lk.15. Contrasted to the forgiveness of the father was the nasty response of the brother in the same passage. There are many of you who simply will not forgive or let go of some past failure from someone with whom you were once close. In some sad cases, they have tried to make things right and yet you refuse to allow that to happen. Almost always this unwillingness to forgive has manifested itself into you becoming one nasty pain in the neck (and other places) to pretty much everyone. You see friend, when you are not eager to forgive, in those instances, usually the real foundational issue is not with the other person: it's with you! Fortunately for you, God stands ready to forgive you even for your unwillingness to forgive others. For you who are listing off all the self-righteous reasons why you are the exception to this rule and thus are not compelled to forgive, let me remind you how serious God takes this matter of not forgiving those who fail us, *"But if you do not forgive men, then your Father will not forgive your transgressions."* (Mt. 6:15).

Concluding Thought: You typically know when someone is not really your friend on at least two occasions. The first is when they won't admit to others that you are their friend (even when with their other set of lips, they tell you they are). The second is when "they" simply will not forgive you. They might be, on rare occasions friendly, but they are not your friend. I would suggest you move on and focus on your real friends. They will be the ones who are standing with you and not embarrassed to stand beside you! Why? Well, as Solomon puts it, "a friend loves at all times." Thanks to you all who have been my true friends! You are deeply loved.

Straight Ahead! JT

59

The Abundant Life

"Jesus therefore said to them again, 'Truly, truly, I say to you, I am the door of the sheep. All who came before Me are thieves and robbers, but the sheep did not hear them. I am the door; if anyone enters through Me, he shall be saved, and shall go in and out, and find pasture. The thief comes only to steal, and kill, and destroy; I came that they might have life, and might have it abundantly. (Jn. 10:7-10)

Jesus desires for us to have an abundant life. Despite the sad teaching of popular TV preachers, this does not mean we will avoid pain, struggles, and even occasional seasons of discouragement. There is nothing wrong with being down and even defeated. Understand this, if you are defeated, know that you don't have to stay there. An example of that is found in Lk. 22:62. Peter has failed Christ by denying Him. He is low, overwhelmed with the reality of his own failure.

In Peter's case, Jesus forgives and restores him with the use of a question found in John 21:15-19. Jesus asks Peter, "*...do you love me?*" with the restored challenge to "*...shepherd*

My sheep." It's powerful to note the change in Peter's life. Not long afterwards we see Peter, in Acts 2:34-38, preaching at Pentecost with a boldness and level of spiritual vitality that is breathtaking. What are some examples of being disheartened? When you continually are looking over your shoulder at past failures, it's easy to develop an "if only" attitude. If only I had not botched that relationship. If only I had not passed up that job. Others are consumed with fears of the future. What about our security as a nation? What kind of a world will our children face? Will I have enough money saved up for our needs in retirement? These kinds of questions can drive us to being consumed with "what if." Others are discouraged with the frustrations of today, "oh my" or "why me?" Often the challenges of health, finances, and family can take the wind out of our walk sails, in life and even in our faith.

The result of all of this is cumulative and it clouds our ability to see God. Here is the good news. We can be delivered from a defeated disposition by remembering God's promises and thoughts about our past, present, and future. Psalms 103 tells us that our transgressions, in the mind of God, are as separated as east is from west. Isaiah 43:25 tells us God chooses to blot out our failures. Hebrews 8:12 explains that for the repentant, God is merciful. Victory also comes because we rest on the promises of God for the future. Matthew 6:34 reminds the child of God he doesn't need to fear the apparent threats of tomorrow.

Finally, when we remember that God is presently watching over each of us and is actively involved in every aspect of our lives, His presence gives me the ability to experience calm even in the midst of the storms we all face. Being a victorious believer doesn't mean you get a pass on struggle, but it does mean that you can have grace and confidence even when you do struggle and this will help you as you journey through your struggles. Press on friends!

Straight Ahead friends! JT

60

Under the Juniper Tree

An alarming rate of the Lord's servants suffer from major discouragement and depression. You will remember that in 1 Kings, chapter 18, Elijah experiences a great victory on Mount Carmel. After this victory, including the execution of the prophets of Baal, God sends rain and helps Elijah win a "foot race" against the chariot of Ahab to Jezreel. After a victorious chapter 18, our hero becomes overwhelmed in chapter 19. Elijah becomes fearful, depressed, and despondent. Notice 1 Kings 19:4. Here the prophet essentially says, "... 'It is enough; now, O LORD, take my life, for I am not better than my fathers.'" Wow, what a change!

The reason I mention this portion of the OT is because it is very instructive for God's servants today. One of the ministries I have been privileged to be a part of is the Institute of Biblical Leadership (www.iblministry.org). One of the things we see all the time is how God's leaders can climb to great heights in ministry only to quickly experience cruel blows, discouragements, and lows. So here is the good news. If this devotional finds you under your juniper tree or in your cave, know that it's okay to not feel okay. God, however, does not want you to stay not okay!

You will notice some very interesting parallels as to the cause and then solution of this type of ministry and life depression. Notice contributing factors to Elijah's depression:

1) – Elijah is going through a major "life" and "ministry-change." From what we can determine here in this portion of 1 Kings, Elijah is going to be transitioning into a new phase of prophetic ministry, namely that of "mentoring" the next major spiritual leader, Elisha. This marks the beginning of the end of Elijah's ministry. When we face times of transition, we are more vulnerable to having a season of discouragement if we focus on the "ending" instead of the "beginning" God is placing before us.

2) – Elijah suffers a major "failed expectation." It seems very apparent from these chapters that Elijah expected Israel to turn back to Jehovah. Not only does that not happen, but also the queen is after his "neck!" This again rings true with those involved in day-to-day life and ministry. How common it is for a pastor to feel like a failure on Monday morning. A Christian school teacher to feel unloved because they struggle with not getting a raise in salary when others in the ministry structure do! A Bible Camp director, when out of a dozen supporting churches, he can only muster up three to help during "clean up week!" A pastor's wife who sees her own sacrifices, her husband's, her children's only to see and hear other ladies in the ministry complain at the smallest of inconveniences. When those "friends" leave your side as partners in the same ministry, it can feel as if a friendship has been betrayed. Often you believe you can say nothing.

3) – Elijah suffers from physical exhaustion. After his victory, he runs all the way to "the entrance of Jezreel." After getting word that the queen is out to get him, he continues his journey all the way to Beersheba where he drops off his servant and then runs fifteen more miles (a day's journey) into the middle of the Negev desert, finds a tree, and essentially collapses. God's servants can suffer all kinds of physiological struggles in the service of ministry. Jesus Himself, after the grueling forty days of temptation in the wilderness, experienced the aid and encouragement of angels (Mt. 4:11). So if Jesus needs encouragement after being physically exhausted in His humanity, how much more will we need God's touch on our bodies in the ebb and flow of vineyard work.

4) – Elijah suffers from emotional and spiritual exhaustion. No question that after the season of spiritual warfare, Elijah was depleted spiritually and emotionally. In Lk. 8:43 and following, we read of an episode in our Lord's ministry where a woman with an issue of blood reached out to Jesus in hopes of healing. He asked the question, *"Who is the one who touched Me?"* The disciples were confused because they were in the midst of a large crowd. Jesus knew that power had departed Him. When you touch those around you in the service of Jesus, you deposit something of yourself in them. Even though we are energized spiritually by Christ and the indwelling Spirit of God, there is an exhaustion that often follows. Sometimes we just need to be "unavailable" for a time to rest and revive our souls.

5) – Elijah suffers from isolation. As we come to 1 kings 19:4, he's all alone under his tree. God never intended for God's children to do their work alone. There might be a few isolated cases in the Scriptures when God's servants did their

work alone, but it's rare. Consider the words of Yahweh in Gen. 2:18, *"It is not good for the man to be alone!"* This wasn't only a statement of the role of a man and a woman in marriage. It was a statement about the importance of community that even the Godhead had experienced. Depression too easily sets in when we isolate ourselves, remain inactive, and begin to ruminate (over-think), and dwell on all our past failures.

The End of the Story—Thankfully, as we read the rest of the chapter, God encourages His servant through his season of anxiety and discouragement in three ways. First, God helps His servant physically with water, sleep, food, and a reasonable life trek to Mt. Horeb. This journey took him forty days, but at only five miles a day as opposed to the running for his life scenario at the beginning of the chapter. Second God helped His servant spiritually. Elijah begins to pray and listen to the voice of God (as we can through God's Word). It's in this section of the passage that Elijah hears God explain that while the prophet feels he's alone, another seven thousand have not bowed the knee to Baal. Lastly, Elijah was aided by the encouragement of a partner in the ministry, Elisha. When we find ourselves under the juniper tree or deep inside our cave, a good place to start is to find the Barnabas' in our life. Let's consider how we can be wiser in our personal health choices, spiritual disciplines, and ensure that our relationships are now and continue to remain healthy. It worked for Elijah!

Straight Ahead friends! JT

Thanks

I wish to simply acknowledge my thanks to God for His unspeakable gift! Nothing is more precious to any of us who know Jesus by way of the gift of eternal life and His forgiveness of our sins through the precious blood of the Lamb! There is nothing to compare to our "great salvation!" (Hebrews 2:3).

I wish to thank my precious wife Toni Lee Carmack Tetreau for twenty-six years of love, partnership, and marriage. Toni has been my better-half in ministry through the ups and downs, the victories and heart-aches. We have walked together in the service of the King and I'm thankful for that.

Thanks to my three sons. Jonathan, Jeremy, and Joshua, who are all headed into life, choosing different vocations and ministering at different levels, each with an eye for leveraging their work for God's purposes.

I'm thankful for godly parents and grandparents who modeled the self-discipline of Scripture and prayer. Over the years, I've watched as their devotional life was the backbone that carried them through the ups and downs of life.

Thanks to the dear supporting folks at the church where I have pastored for nearly two decades here in Gilbert, AZ. Thanks to Southeast Valley Bible Church (www.sevbc.org). Your support for my ministry has been a humbling thing to watch all these years. Thanks also to the supporting staff and family of the Institute of Biblical Leadership (www.iblministry.org) that allows me to serve them a handful of days a month as part-time staff overseeing IBL ministry in the Western United States.

Thanks to the friends who are always there for me. Your encouragement and faithfulness is a life-blessing. Thanks to the friends who have helped with the proof-reading and editing of this project. That had to have been a labor of love.

Finally, thanks to you who will read this devotional with an "open palm" heart. This is a heart that is open to God's direction in your life and God changing you, versus having a "closed palm" heart. This heart is like a fist; the mind has been made up and there is no desire to allow God to use His Word to bring needed growth and life and change. I pray that this devotional will bring encouragement and healing where and when it's needed. You are loved, my friend.

--Straight Ahead! *Pastor Joel*

About the Author

Dr. Joel Tetreau has served in vocational ministry for nearly 27 years. Presently he serves as lead pastor of *Southeast Valley Bible Church* (www.sevbc.org) in Gilbert, AZ. He also serves as the Western Regional Coordinator of the Institute of Biblical Leadership (www.iblministry.org). Joel is a member of the IFCA International and has taught at the undergrad and graduate level in Bible and Theology. Joel studied at the International Baptist College and Seminary, Detroit Baptist Theological Seminary, Calvary Baptist Theological Seminary, Jerusalem Center of Biblical Studies and Central Baptist Theological Seminary. He has formerly belonged to the Evangelical Theological Society. He has served several ministries as a board member. Joel is the author of *"The Pyramid and the Box: The Decision-Making Process in a Local New Testament Church"* (Wipf and Stock Publishers, 2013). He has spoken at numerous leadership conferences and has worked with Christian leaders of various churches, fellowship groups and ministries around the world. He is married to the love of his life Toni and together they have their home in Gilbert, AZ. Their three sons Jonathan (and his wife Brittany), Jeremy, and Joshua are very involved in music and ministry. Joel loves to bike and travel. He can be reached at jtetreau@cox.net

Made in the USA
Columbia, SC
12 June 2018